Gordon Wallace

Gordon Wallace has been a freelance writer for over 30 years.

He is the author of *'Minding My Own Business'* a book about young entrepreneurs published by Lang Syne Publishing and sponsored by Scottish Enterprise.

A radio documentary *'Just a Few Lines'* based on the letters of a First World War soldier was scripted by him and broadcast by BBC Radio on two occasions and given a Sony Award for best programme in its class. His short story *'Picture in a Junk Shop'* has also been broadcast by BBC Radio 4.

He was commissioned to write about the human side of running a business which was then animated and put up on an educational website. He has scripted a one-act play performed at the Edinburgh Link Festival and his work has appeared in a range of newspapers and journals including the Herald, The Scotsman, TES and the Architects Journal. For two years he contributed a regular column to his local newspaper. His poetry has appeared in the English-language weekly, Athens News

The success of his First World War radio programme encouraged him to write, *'Sonny'*. Two other works of non-fiction are currently underway, these being *'Food for Thought'* (the way food has been depicted and its symbolism in fine art) and a biography of the artist, Mary Louise Coulouris.

For 12 years he was Director of Enterprise for a large city-centre college where he worked with businesses in the art & design sector, print and publishing.

Gordon Wallace is a Churchill Fellow and work for his thesis was carried out in the United States. He was married to the artist, Mary Louise Coulouris, daughter of Hollywood actor George Coulouris. He lives in Linlithgow near Edinburgh, but spends much of the year on the Greek island of Hydra.

Introduction by Philip Algar

Many books chronicle the horrors of the First World War but few reveal the insight shown by Gordon Wallace. After early confirmation of the death of Sonny, the main character, from Manchester, he recounts the story of the youth confronted with the lunacies of war. Many histories are self-serving offerings from generals and politicians, keen to show themselves in a better light than their actions warranted. Churchill claimed that history would treat him favourably, because he would write it. Using some of Sonny's letters, Wallace tells a story so well researched, so vivid, so candid and so realistic, it is difficult to believe that he was not there himself in those muddy, bloody battles where the participants knew not whether they would survive that day.

Not content with merely vilifying Field Marshall Douglas Haig, Wallace traces his background which influenced but did not excuse his cavalier stance towards losing so many men for so little. The stubborn, Haig, seemingly knowingly, scheduled battles when the weather was unfavourable. In 1918, if families wanted a personal message on relatives' graves, the cost, of 3.5 old pence per letter, was, literally, prohibitive for many. Haig received £100,000 tax free for his efforts.

The immediate patriotic enthusiasm for the war, and the need to sustain it, was promoted by the War Propaganda Bureau and the War Office Press Bureau. Truth was an early casualty and propaganda was rampant a century ago.

Anxious to avoid public concern at the rate of casualties prompted the repatriation of victims during the night and only details of officers killed were published. Much was done through the Defence of the Realm Act. "The fact that DORA was the most invidious piece of law-making ever to have blighted Britain allowed the propagandist to avoid what was really happening on the war front and to distort the truth through deliberate misreporting of events".

The need to recruit more volunteers for military service led to the formation of PALS battalions. It was thought that men would be more likely to serve if they were with others from their own city. The incentives to volunteer were conjured up by committee members who had commercial and often vested interests in "offering" new recruits. As the slaughter continued, the idea failed as remnants of different groups had to be combined. As the war staggered on, commenting on the ambulances on the streets of Manchester, taking casualties to hospital, Wallace notes that the "enthusiasm waned and any outward signs of patriotic fever rapidly cooled to the silent sweat of trepidation and fear".

This book is not just about a young man, who, like millions of others, was killed without really knowing why he was involved. Wallace writes fluently about life in Manchester in the early days of the last century and the grim existence in the trenches. The story is weaved into a coherent and compelling whole. This is a humane, passionate, penetrating and valuable contribution to understanding the travails of the millions who were sucked and suckered into a conflict that neither was the war to end all wars and which did not produce a land fit for heroes.

SONNY
The Truth Between the Lines

Gordon Wallace

To Luke + Claire

Light + Love
gordon.

peakpublish

Peakpublish
An imprint of Peak Platform
New Bridge
Calver
Hope Valley
Derbyshire S32 3XT
First published by Peakpublish 2012

Copyright Gordon Wallace
All rights reserved
The moral right of the author has been asserted
Cover Design Ian Orange

Printed at svanprinters, India (www.svanprinters.com)
No part of this publication may be reproduced, stored in a retrieval system, or transmitted, in any form or by any means, electronic, mechanical, photocopying, recording or otherwise, without the prior permission of the publishers.

A CIP catalogue record for this book is available from the British Library

ISBN: 978-1-907219-29-0
www.peakplatform.com

Dedication

To those who died and continue to die in wars waged far from home.

Acknowledgements

For a book like this I owe many debts to many people too numerous to mention here. I thank them for putting their knowledge and expertise within easy reach of my pen.

Many thanks also to Eric and Dorothy not to mention the redoubtable Mildred Beech, and for the unflagging support of my late wife, Mary Louise.

Most of all I owe Geraldine and Sridhar for their courage and professionalism. Without them the ink would never have marked the paper.

>This much we know, yet still we wait,
>In shadows cast by things unsaid.
>Amid the shaky pulse of faith,
>Whose sterile virtues claimed the dead?

(From 'After the Planes' by Gordon Wallace)

Foreword

In some ways this might be seen as the story of a 'nobody' - the tale of a man who died young, left little to posterity and whose very existence has now passed from all living memory. Yet at the time of his death the highest in the land were expressing their regrets and every year since people in many parts of the world pay tribute to his life and recall the shocking circumstances which took it away. There is reason to believe these annual remembrances will continue: so whatever other changes time brings there is little chance of our 'nobody' being entirely forgotten.

Joseph Prince Boothroyd – known to his family and friends as 'Sonny' – was within a few months of his 22nd birthday when he was killed. Who his killer was will always remain a mystery, although even if he had been caught no charges would have been brought against him. At the time, ending another man's life was seen as an accomplishment rather than a crime, a deed of duty rather than an act of murder. However, there is good reason to speculate that the man who killed Sonny didn't know for certain that he'd done so. He may even have suffered the loss of his own life shortly afterwards because at the time instant death, often followed by makeshift burial, was commonplace – something few of us today can reflect on free from feelings of revulsion and disbelief.

A fortnight before he died, Sonny had written to his mother thanking her for some food she had sent him and wishing her a *'Bright and Prosperous New Year.'* The letter – one of just 20 to survive – was the last one he ever wrote. Extracts from his letters appear in this book, providing a few fragments as to what sort of person he was. That he had a lucky streak which carried him relatively unscathed through a succession of nightmarish-events will be obvious to anyone following this account of his brief adult life. That lucky streak, as lucky streaks tend to do, ran out on him the day he came face to face with his killer.

Before embarking on what was to be the long and exhausting journey leading to his death, Sonny Boothroyd had spent his life within the clasp of a large working-class family in Manchester, and on leaving school had become the employee of a grocery chain with a branch just a few steps away from his front door. In deciding to be a shop assistant he'd eschewed any idea of following his father, Joseph, into an industrial occupation – a decision that would have pleased his mother, but fail to gain his father's endorsement. In Sonny's day becoming a shop assistant was regarded as having aspirations to a better life, one that would equate eventually with the higher status given to those employed in Manchester's booming commercial life. For most working class fathers however, ambitions of that sort might well have been viewed as a son getting above himself and this probably explains why Joseph Boothroyd fails to get a mention in any of Sonny's letters.

With his fairish-hair, slight physique and blue eyes set in a fresh complexion, Sonny would have been likeable to the women shopping at his grocery store: but there is nothing to suggest he had a sweetheart, someone who might have swum to the forefront of his mind as the dangers around him multiplied. There can be little doubt he found the opposite sex as intriguing as any young man, but they were a mystery yet to be unravelled. Certainly, the only females present on the day he left Manchester for the last time were his mother and two sisters. As they saw him off at the railway station they noticed how he moved down the platform without looking back and rolled away without as much as a farewell wave from the open carriage window. Perhaps, like them, he didn't want to make a fuss and was intent on concealing his own emotional state. It was a time after all, when sad farewells were far more common than happy, welcoming returns.

In preparation for what lay ahead of him, Sonny had been leant upon never to show his emotions or even look dispirited. Those were things you did in private or preferably not at all. Only the virtues of pride, courage and enthusiasm for what he was about to face were considered proper and by April 1915, in swapping his grocer's apron for a suit of khaki, Sonny was ready to do his bit as a volunteer soldier in the First World War. *'For God, For King & For Country'* was the inscription embossed on the notepaper he'd use to write his letters home but like most of his comrades, Sonny Boothroyd wasn't so much a soldier than an ordinary citizen put in uniform and handed a rifle with which to win a war. Much was expected of him he was told, and much was the weight that would be put on his narrow, youthful shoulders. In the end however, it became a burden too onerous to carry......

Chapter 1

It is Boxing Day, 1917, and Sonny Boothroyd is preparing for a march through the freezing Flanders dusk. As a soldier of the Manchester Regiment he has already endured 18 months of gruelling encounters with the First World War. No sooner had he arrived on the Western Front from his training camp in England than the Battle of the Somme was upon him. He survived only to experience several months of equally desperate combat around the devastated area of Arras. Then came that, *'Carnival of Death'* – Passchendaele – a battle so lately concluded and to so little effect that only the most blinkered observer can justify it ever having been fought at all. However, savage and convulsive though these battles have been they've failed to make heroes of the generals who ordered them and have added nothing more than a blood-soaked comma to the dismal narrative of the war so far. The shells still shriek, gas still gathers on the battlefields and for Sonny Boothroyd there is still one more murderous skirmish to come.

Today, his unit, the 19th Battalion of the Manchester Regiment has been tasked to carry out what soldiers call *'The Hate'* - the process of relieving men of another regiment in the frontline trenches. It's a hazardous operation at any time, but at dusk and again at dawn the risks multiply. The Germans, whose own defences lie just a few hundred yards away from the British frontline, are more likely to make a trench raid under cover of darkness, one objective being to take prisoners from men newly arriving at the front. Such prisoners, especially if they include officers, have been known to carry valuable intelligence information, or under duress might be persuaded to reveal Allied plans for imminent attack. There have been reports that across Sonny's section of the Western Front trench raids are increasing in frequency, and after the chaos wrought by Passchendaele the Allied defences are not what they should be. The barb-wire entanglements are anything but complete, and the Germans are exploiting the gaps with their usual ruthless intensity.

In a few hours time Sonny will be ordered to, '*Stand To*', a command that will have him clambering on to the fire-step of a frontline trench, fully armed and bayonet fixed, ready to detect any signs of enemy activity amongst the debris and devastation of no-man's land. For an hour after midnight this will be his prime responsibility, though following that will be stints of sentry duty with up to five of his fellow-infantrymen. Apart from a few short periods of fitful sleep in what passes for a dugout, the sentry post will constitute his entire world throughout the hours of darkness. Tomorrow night, unless detailed for other tasks, he will be required to perform the same routine again.

As he musters for the march, Sonny is aware that Christmas Day has come and gone without any semblance of Yuletide cheer. Yesterday he was told his battalion's Christmas dinner had been postponed until the 29th of December when he and his unit are due to be relieved and returned to their base camp at the rear. He recalls hearing that Christmas in the trenches hadn't always been subject to such delays. Three years back, during the first Christmas of the war, troops from opposite sides in the conflict had taken it upon themselves to call a halt to the fighting and meet in no-man's land to shake hands and exchange small gifts. Food and drink had changed hands and cigarettes and chocolate were given and received. Once the rum and schnapps had been swallowed, much laughter and hearty backslapping had followed. To anyone not fully acquainted with the situation, there might not have been a war going on at all....

Long before 1917 arrived however, such events had disappeared into the battlefield mud along with most of the soldiers who'd participated in them. Today, *'fraternising with the enemy'* was a punishable offence ending any chance of that first Christmas truce being repeated. It was arguable anyway if soldiers like Sonny Boothroyd had the desire, never mind the means, to mark Christmas on the battlegrounds. Morale had sunk so low that an anxious military had begun monitoring it through closer reading of a soldier's mail at the time of its censoring. As the war ground grimly on morale declined even further as the supply of food and the energy it provided, both dwindled. Even the rum issue had gone from a tot per day to one every eight days except for troops waiting to go into action. The inebriating effects of alcohol – the subject of much disapproval by the temperance movement at home – had from the start of the war been used to embolden men waiting to go over the top. Afterwards, in its other role as a palliative, it was administered to soldiers whose wounds were driving them to an otherwise painful death.

As he waits for the command to start marching, Sonny falls in remembering what it was like this time of the year in his native Manchester. *'It's a place I'd sooner be'*, he'd written in a recent letter to his mother, *'as there is not so many shells flying about there'*. Yet a part of him is almost relieved at not being home for Christmas. He wonders what his family would make of him now after such a long absence, and how they would react to his appearance after all this time in the hellholes of war. For one thing he looks older than someone his age might be expected to look. His hair is beginning to grey at the temples: his eyes peer out from sunken sockets: and the pallor of his cheeks is mitigated only where the straps of his gas helmet has bruised and reddened the skin. Beneath his greatcoat, buttoned to the neck against the winter chill, the effects of a shrapnel wound continues to pain him and in his boots the process of 'trench foot' – the slowly rotting flesh that has become the scourge of so many soldiers – refuses to subside. As he girds himself with the weaponry, tools and equipment needed for the relief operation, there are few signs of the teenager who'd once written of his eagerness to be gone, doing his bit for King and Country……

FOR GOD, FOR KING & FOR COUNTRY

Pte. J. Boothroyd 18452
26th Reserve Battalion, The Manchester Regiment
Prees Heath Training Camp, Salop
February 1916

 Dear mother...just a line to let you know I am still alive and in the pink. I got the parcel you sent last week, but can you send me something along as I am a bit short. I expected coming home this week, but it did not come off. There has been a big draft of our men sent to Flanders. I could not get in it, but I shall be in the next lot. It is a fine place. Hope you are all well.
 Sonny.

'Be a Man!' the billboards had screeched when war was declared. *'It Is More Blessed To Go Than Be Pushed.'* Lord Kitchener, the Minister of War and just the man to do the pushing if it came to it, appeared on posters declaring *'Your Country Wants You!'* his forefinger like a blunt bayonet pointed at any lily-livered individual skulking past on the pavement.

 In Sonny Boothroyd's Manchester, what was soon being described in the newspapers as the, *'fever of patriotism,'* was no less virulent than in other towns and cities in the land. Though still below the minimum age for enlistment, Sonny watched as cheering crowds gathered in the streets, waving flags and hoisting banners exhorting men to volunteer for the First World War. If patriotism had always paid dividends in the eyes of those who governed Britain, then according to reports, these dividends now vastly exceeded anything seen in the past.

Even blowing your nose was regarded as patriotic providing you did it using a handkerchief designed as the union jack.

Despite being 'neutral' prior to hostilities breaking out the city's main newspaper, the Manchester Guardian quickly changed its stance once the war was underway. Reviewing the march past of Manchester's first volunteer soldiers it said:

The people who cheered and the people who marched were not spectators and a spectacle. They were kin in the truest sense, and every eligible man who watched the City Battalions swing by must have felt it an incongruous thing that he was not on the other side of the barrier.

Soon, the country's other newspapers began expressing similar sentiments and it became something of a competition to see who could influence recruiting figures most through patriotic headlines and reports.

Politicians also closed ranks, their erstwhile differences set aside. MPs of all parties joined with trade union leaders and local luminaries to demonstrate their unalloyed support for the conflict. Even sections of the suffragette movement, for long a thorn in the side of government, managed to get the title of its weekly magazine changed to *'Britannia'* and continued to vilify pacifists, conscientious objectors and any other backsliders brought to their notice. Just a handful of people struck a note of defiance but succeeded only in singling themselves out for particularly vicious forms of opprobrium. Cast adrift on the waves of war hysteria sweeping Parliament, the leader of the yet-youthful Labour Party, Ramsey MacDonald, did the only thing he claimed his conscience would allow and resigned from his post.

However, it was the local news-sheets who really undertook the job of selling recruitment to those living in the areas where they circulated. Men were reported as *'besieging recruitment centres'* in every port and parish, in many cases deserting work and wages to put themselves forward for enlistment. It was however, a distorted view of the situation as *'disappointing'* recruitment figures were soon to show. The 'besieging' had more to do with a shortage of recruiting centres (many places only had one initially) than the fires continuing to burn in patriotic breasts.

Other than Ramsey MacDonald, a few other dissenting voices were heard briefly above the pro-war clamour. Shortly, the playwright, George Bernard Shaw, was reported as advising soldiers to shoot their officers and return home and when posed the question *'Daddy, what did you do in the Great War?'* the miner's union leader, Robert Smillie, replied *'I tried to stop the bloody thing, my child!'* These views were met with outrage by their opponents who were all for having them deported or tried for treason, something that would have been possible at the time under the terms of the Defence of the Realm Act (DORA) which had been rushed through Parliament without debate in the first weeks of the war. However, plans to boost recruitment were already in hand, so the draconian DORA was left for another time when 'troublemakers' and 'appeasers' had to be more sternly dealt with. In the meantime the state's response to those who refused to fight was either a prison sentence or forced labour in the munitions industry, although there were cases of conscientious objectors being assigned to the battlefields in 'non-combatant' roles such as stretcher-bearers. The life of a stretcher-bearer on the battlegrounds was known to be short, and it can be assumed that those who appointed them to such duties knew exactly what they were doing...

There is little way of knowing how much Sonny Boothroyd was influenced by these events. He was at the time a shop assistant and seen as being destined for better things. His future, he'd been encouraged to believe, lay outside the realm of oppositional politics and the ceaseless class antagonisms of his times. Like the mass of British people of course he didn't have a vote, so his views on anything were ultimately of little interest to whoever sat in Parliament, reputedly on his behalf. For Sonny life held out prospects of advancement beyond the reach of most young men from working class backgrounds, if only because being a shop assistant was regarded as an occupation hovering on the boundaries of becoming respectably middle-class. This view owed little to the Victorian belief of 'self-improvement' but to fundamental shifts in the economy, shifts that were causing wholesale changes in the composition of the workforce. Being a shop assistant, though yet to achieve the status of those like clerks and warehousemen in Manchester's commercial sector, was steadily moving in that direction. As a marker of how far it had progressed, shop assistants were now often referred to as 'clerks', while those who followed their father's footsteps into industry remained, as always, mere 'factory hands'.

Ahead of him now however, as the light begins fading over the dreary landscape of Flanders, Sonny contemplates a quite different route from the one mapping him through life in the retail sector. It is a route with few reliable indicators, and he would choose to have it go anywhere other than the frontline. Shortly after traversing a stretch of open road, he will veer off into trenches that are little more than shallow indentations in the sodden earth. Digging here, even by a few inches, causes the groundwater to bubble up and wash over the wooden duckboards soldiers walk on. In the diminishing light it is easy for a man to lose his footing and fall headlong, especially today as the temperature drops and occasional flurries of snow make the surfaces even more treacherous.

Around him the men of the 19th Manchesters are growing increasingly quiet. Holy Night may well have come and gone, but silent night is about to establish itself across the entire sector. By order, all talk is to be rationed and gradually reduced to whispers as the frontline approaches: and any unnecessary noise will receive a strong reprimand. If the enemy...so the argument goes... were to be alerted by noise during the changeover, then any raiding party circulating in no-man's land would have a focus for their endeavours. Familiar though this belief is (troops on both sides know frontline relieves are always done under the cover of darkness), it serves only to increase the tension in men already apprehensive about the vulnerability of their position.

The idea that talk could cost lives however isn't the one dominating Sonny's thoughts as he collects his gear and shoulders his rifle. Like every other man in his unit, the only question worth considering has no real need for verbal expression. As the order to begin marching arrives, he thinks...*someday this whole bloody business will end: but meanwhile how do I get through till tomorrow without getting hurt?* All his training and preparations for war...all the military discipline and battle rehearsals he's undergone can't, unfortunately, provide anything in the way of a meaningful answer and as if he didn't know already, there isn't a soldier within the entire compass of the Western Front who can. ……

Chapter 2

The First World War – in case you need reminding - began in the late-summer of 1914 and ended officially with the signing of an armistice in November 1918. History records that Britain and her allies were victorious over Germany and the Central Powers: but in reality it was a pyrrhic victory. Considering the massive casualties sustained by both sides, it could be seen as little more than a damnable draw. People who celebrated the end of the war did so more out of a sense of relief than anything else. When the *'lamps which had gone out all over Europe'* were re-lit, they revealed such scenes of devastation that few people felt it had all been worth it. Long before the conflict shuddered to an end the landscape of people's minds had begun mirroring the landscape of the battlefields, and there was hardly a family in the land who hadn't in some way been grievously damaged by it.

According to opinion at the time, the First World War was not expected to last for any more than a few months. *'All Over By Christmas!'* was the message directed at potential volunteers and their families, fostering the notion that few would be required to risk death and injury and it would all be finished quicker than it took a recruit to learn how to salute his commanding officer. Instead, the war ground on for four-and-a-quarter years. Presumably there were reasons for getting the arithmetic wrong and making what was a horrendous miscalculation: on the other hand, maybe not. Perhaps there were people who understood from the outset this was going to be one of the longest, not to say costliest conflicts in history until that time. If so, they kept their opinions to themselves.

The cost of the First World War in human flesh and blood is what they say roots it in our collective consciousness where it has remained for almost a century: unless of course, like Field Marshall Sir Douglas Haig, you remain largely unmoved by the loss of life on a stupendous scale. *'The nation must be taught to bear losses,'* he declared on the eve of the Battle of the Somme. *'The nation must be prepared to see heavy casualty lists.'* For once the Commander-in-Chief of British forces on the Western Front got it right. On the first day of the Somme, 20,000 soldiers died in a hail of German machine-gun fire and artillery bombardments. A further 40,000 were wounded. By the time the war was over 8 million people had lost their lives and 30 million others had been wounded or mentally deranged by their experiences on the battlegrounds, effectively robbing them of the chance of leading a normal life afterwards. When King George V, speaking at a cemetery in Flanders after the First World War said, *'We can truly say that the whole circuit of the earth is girdled with the graves of our dead',* he was deferring as much to the facts as to those of his subjects who'd died in the conflict.

If for no other reason than the appalling casualty figures, people have always felt they had a right to know not just what caused the First World War, but who it was who prevailed on young men like Sonny Boothroyd to volunteer for it. The fact they still seek meaningful answers almost a century later suggests they haven't been entirely convinced by what they've been told down through the decades.

Historians and pundits alike – often taking their cues from each other – seem to have dealt with every conceivable aspect of the war, ranging from the machinations of politicians and the ineptitude of military commanders, to the destructive capacity and sheer firepower on both sides of the conflict. Even before the First World War ended the focus was already shifting away from causes to conduct, from identifying those within the nation's towns and cities who had been responsible for sending men to their deaths to tactical questions about how the war was fought and why it wasn't ended sooner. In a sense it is like a doctor telling his patient he is seriously ill without explaining how his diseased condition came about. The same tendency, you might think, continues regarding wars being fought in the present time.

If everything that's been written about the First World War was to be laid end-to-end, it would probably stretch further than the 450 miles of frontline trenches dug by the troops on the Western Front. Outside of religious books and bodice-ripping romances you might wonder if anything has generated more text than the First World War. However, even if we were able to achieve the impossible by assimilating it all would we then be able to answer the questions that matter - why it was fought in the first place, and who should we see as being responsible for sentencing so many to such savagery and death? The answer is probably no. Such issues are rarely, if ever, discussed. Just as the grave has closed around those who perished in the conflict, it has also closed around those who sent them to their deaths. Although the remains of the First World War are regularly exhumed for further examination, the skeletons of those mostly responsible stay undisturbed. It is wrong to pass the sins of fathers on to their children, but even the descendants of those who sent young men like Sonny Boothroyd to the trenches are unaware (perhaps blissfully so) of what their relatives did. After all, they were men and women of substance at the time and continued to be so until the end of their own days. So, just like spokespeople in the current age who appear on our television screens to explain why this war and that is deemed to be necessary, we end up like the confused patient - left to make the diagnoses for ourselves.

Chapter 3

The first part of Sonny's march to the frontline takes him along a section of road that by normal standards on the Western Front is in reasonably good condition. Thanks to the dogged efforts of the army's Labour Corps, most of the shell holes gouged-out by German artillery fire have been filled-in so that the surface is now able to support heavier volumes of traffic travelling between key points behind the lines. As they make their way forward, the men of Manchester's 19th battalion have to be alert to the constant movement around them. Coming from behind are interminable convoys of horse-drawn and motorised vehicles carrying supplies and munitions. Careering past in the opposite direction are empty wagons, their drivers barely visible behind swathes of clothing worn to offset the growing chill. As the day dwindles under a steel-grey sky the traffic flow increases, the assumption being that in the gathering gloom a lull in enemy shelling is more-likely than in daylight. That's the hope anyway even if it often evaporates in a sudden storm of shrapnel.

When this part of Flanders was first fought over by the Romans, Julius Caesar understood only too well the need for withdrawing his troops to winter quarters. In 1917 however, such wisdom is yet to be embraced by those who give soldiers their orders on the Western Front. Locked in a stasis of mud and water, the First World War has long proved incapable of any significant movement: yet men are expected to go on acting as though it had. Recently, at the battle for Passchendaele, they'd been left floundering hopelessly and helplessly in the mire, as much victims of the battlefield itself as the enemy's guns. Countless numbers died after falling into flooded shell holes or seeking cover in craters lined with suffocating mud. Their remains are never likely to be recovered and occasionally Sonny spots a waterproof sheet, issued for a soldier's protection, rising from the poisonous depths to show how it finally became his shroud. On both sides of no-man's land, 'military intelligence' has now proved to be the ultimate oxymoron.

As they plod forward, often in single column formation, the 19th battalion leave behind them the Hedge Street Tunnels – a complex of fortifications they've been detailed to improve and extend since arriving there from their base camp on December 23rd. Strictly speaking these ought to be known as the 'Hooge' tunnels being near a shell-blasted village of that name. However, the army has license to name places as they see fit, continuing the colonial tradition of giving places English names as a statement of possession, even if possession here has come at a high price in human lives. Consequently, Hooge has become Hedge and the closest town – the equally devastated textile centre of Ypres – has become 'Wipers.' There's a joke doing the rounds that, 'Wipers' has been so named because of the rain that falls here with relentless monotony: even the horses, they say, need wipers rather than blinkers to get around.

Recently though, after the horrors of Passchendaele a more macabre slant has been put on the name. So many have fallen here since the war began that entire battalions have disappeared, literally 'wiped-off' the roster of available fighting units.

Ahead of him now Sonny can see the hunched figures of his comrades as they pick their way towards where they will leave the road and enter the first set of communication trenches which link to the frontline but their names and in some instances even their faces are barely familiar to him. At the time of his enlistment and before the Somme, this had been far from being the case. Men who'd been little more than a dim outline in the dark Sonny had been able to identify without much trouble. He knew by sight almost everyone in his company of 200 men, and beyond that many others belonging to the battalion. When they talked together it was as often as not in accents enriched with the idioms acquired in childhood within the boundaries of their native Lancashire.

This aptitude for being able to put names to faces had come about due to the circumstances of volunteer recruitment that had prevailed in the early rounds of the war. Friends had been encouraged to enlist with friends, employees with fellow-employees. Men from middle-class backgrounds and those who aspired to be part of that social stratum were the main targets. Those who belonged to the same church, the same sports club, who'd attended the same school or youth organisation, who drank, smoked, bantered, laughed and spent much of their time together were recruited together with the promise of being placed in the same battalion. The battalions themselves were raised locally, and in the beginning paid for out of local subscriptions. Flowing naturally from this mode of recruitment, the title bestowed on these components of Lord Kitchener's new volunteer army, was derived from a spirit of familiarity and fellowship: they were called the 'PALS' battalions.

The moving force in getting the PALS regiments together was an army general, Sir Henry Rawlinson, though responsibility for recruiting to them was soon placed in the hands of civilians – men seen as having influence in their localities and therefore better equipped to bring the PALS idea to fruition. In the city of Manchester, likewise in Liverpool, the man chosen to spearhead the PALS campaign was the super-wealthy 'Uncrowned King of Lancashire', Lord Derby. In complete accord with the idea that men would be more willing to volunteer if they were given assurances they would not find themselves '...*in a battalion with unknown men as their companions.*', Lord Derby took to his task with zeal. Better than most he understood the potential of an appeal unashamedly directed at the aspiring middle-class sections of the population where attitudes to the lower orders, including those making up the regular army were already long-established.

But if the PALS idea was rooted in Britain's class-ridden society, it also had a history stretching back to a time when the country's armed forces was dependant on attracting a high quota of rough diamonds. The Duke of Wellington, referring to his troops at Waterloo, spoke of them as having been recruited from sections of the population described as *'the scum of the earth'* – an underclass of social misfits who made up much of the army's foot-soldiers. Among them were men who were illiterate, unemployable in anything but the roughest occupations, and whose only future pointed to service with the military as an alternative to a prison sentence. This didn't sit at all well with prospective middle-class PALS and their parents at the time of the First World War, and recruitment at the start of the conflict, despite the public displays of patriotism, was sluggish and below what the generals deemed necessary. Something had to be done and soon was: but if the element of cunning which lay at the heart of the PALS idea proved to be a runaway success, it also brought with it unimaginable heartache.

On the first day of the Somme, as a result of the horrendous casualties sustained by the PALS battalions, the idea of friends serving with friends was as dead as the soldiers who'd perished within its conceit. The huge gaps in fighting personnel that occurred were hurriedly filled by men drafted in from other regiments, regiments which themselves had been decimated by equally ruinous battles. These replacement drafts were strangers to Sonny, soldiers who appeared reluctantly from units that belonged to places far from his native Manchester. They were also a different sort of soldier, abidingly tired and ill-tempered...conscripts, bristly with complaints and a sullen contempt for their officers. They were as far away from the PALS view of the war as they were from their own homes and families.

Sonny was on close terms with few of them, though conditions on the Western Front in 1917 hardly lent themselves to making lasting friendships. A friend made one day could easily be the corpse you were detailed to bury the next. Long before Passchendaele came along the glue which held the PALS together had melted and rapidly disappeared in the heat of other battles. '*Dear mother,'* Sonny had written after surviving the Battle of the Somme. *'Just a line to let you know...there is a lot of my pals gone west these last few days, lads I enlisted with.'* Later, he wrote again *'It seems just a case of waiting while your turn comes.'*

To either side of him now as he moves forward, the debris of war litters the landscape. On one side are several broken gun limbers and abandoned field guns: on the other, burned out motor vehicles and other equipment rendered useless by shell fire or the ingress of mud and water. In between, and still in harness, lie the carcasses of slain animals – horses and mules, polluting the air with their own unmistakable stench of decay. There is also gas to worry about: not only the chance of a renewed and terrifying attack from the German lines, but the residue from previous bombardments. Mustard gas particularly has the property of lingering and is difficult to detect where it gathers close to the surface of the ground. The damage it inflicts is so malignant a man exposed to it either chokes to death or is incapacitated enough to wish perhaps that he had. Either way, it will assuredly render him unfit to fight again.

Never to fight again of course, is a dream Sonny and his comrades cherish more than anything else. It is one of the main sources of talk in the trenches, often the only one. When will it end? Who will finally put a finish to it? The 'lucky bugger' is the soldier who is wounded by enemy fire before even getting out of his trench, although men have been known to commit self-mutilation - deliberately wounding themselves in the hope of being removed from the action and hospitalised, preferably at home in Britain. Given the choice though, most would prefer returning to what they now call 'Blighty' without resorting to any such nihilistic actions.

Going home, getting out, going back to a life which compared to that endured on the flat, painful plains of Flanders seems like a return to the fields of Elysium. Soldiers think about it, talk about it, dream about it. Only those sifting through the content of their letters home notice that few mention how this is to be achieved short of a truce being arranged between the main combatant nations. It appears that hardly anyone, other than the military top brass, is talking about a total victory over the enemy....

Chapter 4

Keeping minds from straying too far from what was needed to achieve victory was the job of government. Moving at the speed of light, they set up the WPB (the War Propaganda Bureau) a few days after war was declared. Lloyd - George, destined to become the country's new prime minister was given overall responsibility for organising the WPB and deciding who would sit on it. At a secret meeting in London a number of carefully chosen candidates were put in a room to discuss how they might contribute to the perceived need to brainwash the public. Among those attending was Arthur Conan Doyle, the creator of Sherlock Holmes, and the author H.G. Wells. Joining them was Hilaire Belloc, G.K. Chesterton, Rudyard Kipling and a man whose fusion of imperial greatness with the game of cricket coalesced memorably in the lines *'Play Up, Play Up, And Play the Game!'* He was Henry (later Sir Henry) Newbolt. The public, totally unaware of this development, went on being oblivious to it and had to wait 25 years before learning anything much about the WPB's personnel and their activities.

One of the specific tasks of the propagandists was to encourage countries not at war to back the Allied position, or at the very least refrain from helping their enemies. At least that's what historians tend to suggest, although in doing so they help put a glossier surface on the WPB's work, reflecting away the consequences of what they did in other ways. Propaganda targeted at the United States for example – a country that steadfastly refused to involve itself with the First World War until 1917 – was quickly recruited by the Americans to justify selling arms and other war materiel to the Allies from which they made considerable fortunes. What is also conveniently overlooked is America's land-grabbing interests. They waited to see how long their rivals on the global scene took to exhaust themselves, and how things might shake-out thereafter to America's advantage. It could be said that America's vision of a 'new world order', and Britain's insistence on having a 'special relationship' with the U.S. were both conceived in the womb of the First World War.

Overseeing the propaganda work of the WPB once it got underway was someone whose name, Charles Masterman, seemed to have been plucked directly from the stories of rugged individualism appearing on the pages of Boy's Own Paper. He was a Christian Socialist and at various times an M.P. – for a while, post-war, the representative of a constituency within the Boothroyd's Manchester. Prior to the First World War breaking out, Masterman had put heavy emphasis on the view that employers who were particularly exploitative of their workers should seek to attune their relationship with them through religion. He also believed in taking moral responsibility for the poor in society, something that led him at one point to a run-down flat in London where he lived for several years with the downtrodden folk he later wrote about in books and essays which espoused his religion-based humanitarian principles. In the main, however, despite his contribution to various pieces of social welfare legislation in Parliament, he advocated *'moral advancement'* and *'spiritual regeneration'* rather than practical solutions to alleviating poverty in society.

On the face of it Masterman seemed the least-likely candidate to fill the top position in a state propaganda machine where the line between fact and fiction, between truth and lies was not just blurred but frequently erased. Morality, you might think would be something dropped off at reception before entering the WPB's offices at Westminster. But Masterman was primarily a journalist and close to the political and literary elite of the country, enjoying a special regard in the eyes of Lloyd George who he'd worked with for many years within the Liberal Party and its administration. In the opinion of historians including Masterman's biographers, his connections in this respect and his natural flair for organising other people were what led to his appointment as head of the WPB, and that his fall from power and death in 1927 mirrored the demise of Liberal England over the same period. Practically no one associates his drift into drugs and alcohol abuse with the impossible task he had of reconciling his religious beliefs with the daily dissimulations he was expected to come up with in his role as propagandist-in-chief.

As the WPB began exerting its influence over what people were told about the war, Masterman was only too pleased to have Mary Humphry Ward added to his collection of propaganda scribes. In many ways they were kindred spirits, linked by an intolerance to anything that challenged the Victorian 'values' they both believed in. Contrary to how she appears in her studio portraits, Humphry Ward was a short, rather grumpy woman who'd arrived in Britain from the colonies as a child, and went on to marry a man who was on the staff of the London Times which in turn provided his wife with a convenient vehicle for her views. The novels she took to writing followed a familiar pattern, her characters appearing as the acme of the values she herself fervently adhered to, including those militating against active feminism.

In 1909, courtesy of space given to her in The Times, she declared that, *'...men who bear the burden of legal, constitutional, financial, military and international problems ought to be left unhampered by the political inexperience of women.'* No record exists of how Humphry Ward proposed addressing this deficit in women's experience, although she was quite willing to become a founding member of the Anti-Suffrage League and be the editor of its monthly review - a journal whose only justification for existing was to debate the very legal and constitutional issues Humphry Ward argued were outside her gender's sphere of intellectual activity.

As soon as war started, Humphry Ward became even more involved in the things she so assiduously advised other women to avoid. At the invitation of Lord Curzon – former Viceroy of India and soon to become a member of the government's inner war cabinet – Humphry Ward took the leading role in the 'Order of the White Feather', an organisation formed with the sole object of shaming seemingly able-bodied civilians into volunteering for the armed services by publicly humiliating them with the award of a white feather. This had extra-significance for

Humphry-Ward since it originated among her fellow-colonialists who, always fond of a wager, were attracted to cock-fighting. A gamecock with white feathers in its tail was regarded as having little fighting spirit, unlike a pure-bred cock whose plumage betrayed no sign of such wanton cowardice. Consequently, a man having a white feather thrust at him in the street was seen to have little courage or masculinity and deserved to be shamed in front of his peers. Feathers, however, were often attached to boys too young for the army, or to those rejected by the military as physically unfit for combat. As a result the white feather brigade had a blissfully short history: in response to public outrage in Manchester and other cities at the grossness of their behaviour, the government stepped in and quietly put an end to them.

It wasn't the end for Humphry Ward however. Though her novels were later to vanish into obscurity the woman herself continued working actively on behalf of the WPB writing propaganda directed at the American market, but only doing so once the government had agreed to compensate her for the *'financial losses'* arising from (amongst other things) *'the pressure of war taxation'* on her income. Her debts, however, were more likely to have arisen from the profligacy of her son Arnold, who was a gambler, a drunkard, and from his schooldays at Eton guilty of misappropriating funds. Ultimately, Humphry Ward's home had to be sold to pay-off Arnold's debts.

Although its remit was to manufacture propaganda, the WPB wasn't seen as having the expertise to handle every aspect of what was needed to keep the truth about the First World War from the people of Britain. Rather late in the day, those around Lloyd George became aware that commissioning a group of established authors, minor novelists and odd-ball poets wasn't measuring up to the job that needed doing. The way newspapers carried reports on the war, for example, was a special area of concern. With few exceptions their unwavering support for the conflict continued: but it was how they proposed reporting it on a day to day basis that worried some people, including those in government.

No matter the rudimentary levels of education in Britain, most of the population could now read as circulation figures for everything from newspapers to pulp fiction magazines proved. In which case what they read about the war was capable of exerting influence over their views on it, especially on key issues like volunteering and the belief that Germany was the wolf waiting at the gate. So even before Masterman had completed his circle of propaganda scribes the government proceeded to create the WOPB – the War Office Press Bureau – as a means of dealing with their concerns.

The role of the WOPB steered more towards censorship than propaganda, though at times Sherlock Holmes himself would have been hard put detecting where the difference lay. A newspaper headline for instance could easily be drawn from the slogan appearing on a wall poster and vice versa. The text of a press report on the other hand could be trawled for slogans suitable for accompanying poster art. The plain fact was that censorship (refraining from telling the whole truth) overlapped considerably with propaganda (ostensibly not telling the truth at all). Not that any of this bothered the appointees of either organisation: both the WPB and WOPB sprang from their traps, feeling this was how they could show their readiness to do their bit for King and Country - in the case of Masterman and Humphry Ward of course, for God as well.

'Belgian child's hands cut off by Germans' was among the first sensationalist headlines spawned by WOPB and appearing in the national newspapers early in the war. Another was *'Belgium's babies stuck on German bayonets'*. None of these allegations of German atrocities, including the claim that they made defensive ramparts from the corpses of their own soldiers, were ever accompanied by anything in the way of underpinning evidence, and any challenge to them was kept well clear of the correspondence columns of the newspapers.

The War Propaganda Bureau likewise went graphic with posters (reproduced in the press) portraying the enemy in ways that must have had the war cabinet's cheers ringing in their ears. One example depicted the enemy as a robed skeleton drinking human blood from a goblet, dribbling much of it down its front until it gathered in a thick vermilion pool at its feet. In case anyone was naïve enough to view this as a comment on the war as a whole, the apparition appeared wearing a spiked Prussian helmet – the Picklehaube.

Not to be outdone the Germans were equally quick off the mark in getting their own propaganda machine rolling. Von Ludendorf's 'clean hands, clean hearts' brigade seized on *'clean water'* as the subject for fostering hatred of the enemy. *'French doctors infect German wells with plague germs'* was the slightly ponderous translation of one newspaper headline. *'German prisoners blinded by Allied captors'* ran another. The real 'blindness' however, was to become that occasioned by the mounting casualty lists – an event newspapers on both sides of the conflict were quite content eventually to leave unreported.

Anyone considering a sustained challenge to the predictable pro-war propaganda produced by the press and WPB, faced a Herculean task that risked alienating them not only from their peers but in some cases from friends and family as well. In the final analysis, even if the propagandists themselves had wanted to deviate from what they were mandated to produce, they would have been at liberty to shrug and point to a piece of legislation that overshadowed and controlled everything they did. That legislation was DORA – the Defence of The Realm Act – something that had been rushed through Parliament without debate in the first week of the war. Don't blame us blame DORA they would have said, holding up their hands as if to show how they were shackled. The fact that DORA was the most invidious piece of law-making ever to have blighted Britain allowed the propagandists to avoid what was really happening on the warfront, or distort the truth through deliberate misreporting of events.

As history has it, DORA was necessary to *'defend the country from possible internal enemies and spies'*, although the most-blinkered historian cannot deny the draconian impact it had on many other aspects of society once it hit the statute book. It gave government executive powers to do just about anything it considered necessary to control what people did and said about the First World War. Neglecting to blackout your windows at night or own a telephone without a permit was the least of it. Land could be requisitioned by the military and local authorities without notice: workers were forbidden to leave certain places of employment during working hours: and employees could be arrested, held without trial, and imprisoned or deported on being found guilty of trying to escape DORA's steely clutches.

As the press lamely pointed out at various times, DORA also controlled what was deemed suitable for publication, and any news thought to be of use to the enemy (food shortages, industrial discontent, casualty figures, etc), and any questions regarding the military's conduct of the war was considered a serious offence subject to the full rigours of the law. In this context the WOPB acted as a clearing house for press reports, though nothing was ever released to Fleet Street before having the fierce eye of Lord Kitchener run over it first. Kitchener also had the power to decide who was to have the task of reporting directly from the battlefields, appointing Ernest Swinton as the British army's official journalist to the Western Front, instructing him to write about *'what he thought was true, not what he knew to be true.'*

No article, Swinton was told, could ever be passed for publication if it said that he'd actually seen what he had written about. Swinton might watch the youth of his homeland being machine-gunned to oblivion, but was obliged to report it only in terms of what might be done to prevent it happening again. Writing under the pseudonym of 'Eyewitness', Swintons' dispatches from the warfront were first censored by Haig's intelligence staff on the Western Front, then further inked over by Kitchener before whatever remained ever reached the newsrooms. Once there, of course, there was no saying what further 'editing' took place or how much re-formulation of copy was indulged in. If Swinton ever got to reading anything he'd penned on the Western Front, he must have done so believing it to have been written by an entirely different journalist to himself.

Decidedly unhappy with this approach to news reporting were the Americans, who relied heavily on British press reports to keep them in touch with how the war was progressing. What were the aspiring land grabbers of that country to make of the censored dispatches they received, dispatches that reported great offensives that appeared to peter out, victories that a few days later seemed somewhat less glorious than first reported? Even if they had been able to read between the lines what significance might they attach to learning that a fairly useless area of blasted ground might well have changed hands a dozen times in the course of one offensive? The pressure to have more factual, more 'helpful' information from the warfront soon began growing on the other side of the Atlantic.

In time, the British duly bowed to this pressure by sending more journalists to the war zones, although the new boys soon found themselves subject to much the same control over their copy as before. Their work was submitted for censoring in the first instance to a fellow newspaperman, C.F. Montagu, who had been a leader writer for the Manchester Guardian in the run up to the war and was connected through his family to the wealthy 'Lancashire Set' that included Lord Derby. Montagu was also the proud possessor of all his own hair, a detail of immeasurably worthless value had he not dyed it black hoping to convince a recruiting officer he was younger than his 47 years and mad keen to volunteer for the army. Closer to being a pensioner than a PAL, the ruse nevertheless worked and he swapped his typewriter for the censor's pencil, left his wife and seven children behind and fulfilled his dream of serving on the Western Front.

The WPB also recruited artists to paint scenes of the battlegrounds, most of which were only put up for public exhibition after the war had finished. Photographers too were commissioned though even stricter control was exercised over what they snapped. It would not have been considered useful to take pictures of limbless boys, or those minus their heads soon after they'd met with their fate. Paul Nash, one WPB artist whose paintings are reckoned to have helped launch the surrealists, said, *'I am not allowed to put dead men in my pictures because dead men do not exist.'* And a fellow artist, Charles Nevinson, struck an even starker note in writing, *'I am no longer an artist. I am a messenger who will bring back word from men who are fighting to those who want the war to go on for ever.'* To this he was to add, *'Feeble and inarticulate will be my message.'*

On posters and personal letters, on pictures and pieces of news doctored for the press, DORA and her odious twins, censorship and propaganda, exerted their state-sanctioned power. They rose like the asphyxiating gas of the battlefields to choke-off any attempts at home or abroad at revealing the truth about the war. By the time conscription was introduced in 1916 however, the efforts of both the WPB and WOPB were proving unequal to the task of keeping the population solidly behind the war effort, and the more-draconian measures embedded in DORA had to be brought into play.

Any challenge based on what had hitherto been regarded as a threat to basic rights and freedoms was firmly put down. In some parts of Britain, unions representing industrial workers had their leaders arrested ostensibly for objecting to female munitions-workers being employed in the factories, although at the heart of the matter lay DORA's proscriptive effects on their movements and organising activities. The result for many of those put before the courts was imprisonment, or else banishment to other towns and cities far from their places of work and areas of influence.

Historians often dismiss DORA's effects by claiming that most people viewed its stern ordinances as unwelcome but necessary, and that only those ignorant of the law ever fell victim to it. They point to the arrests and cautions issued by the police and military saying they mostly arose in cases where people accidentally broke the rules through being unaware of what they were. It's an odd interpretation of what went on in a situation where people were being kept in the dark about the very things the Defence of the Realm Act was designed to conceal from them. Perhaps if people had known more about what DORA was succeeding in doing, they wouldn't have been so accepting of it. How, it might be asked, can it be said people accepted something whose aim was to hide the truth from them and distort the facts?

In the latter stages of the First World War, the man who'd initially accepted responsibility for organising censorship and propaganda, David Lloyd George, told a journalist *'If people really knew [what was going on] the war would be stopped tomorrow: but of course they don't – and can't know. The (news) correspondent doesn't write and censorship wouldn't pass the truth. The thing is horrible and beyond human nature to bear, and I feel I can't go on any longer with the bloody business.'*

This was the Prime Minister and head of the War Cabinet himself talking, presumably at his wits end and plumbing the depths of despair. However, he was soon to recover his equilibrium. The bloody business he referred to, though you would never guess from what appeared in your newspaper, was to continue for some time yet.

Chapter 5

By the time Sonny was old enough to volunteer for the First World War, the 19th battalion of The Manchester Regiment – the army unit he was eventually to join – was already nine months into its preparations for fighting on the Western Front. It had been raised as the '4th City PALS', one of several such battalions raised in Manchester and one of 550 PALS units raised in Britain as a whole. In September 1914, barely a month after war was declared the 4th City PALS had been paraded in front of the Minister for War, Lord Kitchener, and what was described as a large animated crowd of friends, family and well-wishers had then seen them off for further combat-rehearsal outside of the city. This took place a fortnight before Sonny swore his oath of allegiance to the monarch, took that gentleman's money (the 'King's shilling') and went home to wait for his call-up papers. When they arrived he found himself posted to a reserve battalion in Shropshire for training.

Like all battalions of the same provenance, Manchester's 4th City PALS could trace its origins back to General Henry Rawlinson who has been credited with putting the PALS idea in front of his chief Lord

Kitchener. Kitchener was interested because he knew... contrary to what was being said in the press and elsewhere...that the First World War would never be over by Christmas, and that a serious shortfall in recruitment was already beginning to show. His estimate of the number of fighting men needed was 150,000 every month from August 1914 through to the end of the following year: but when recruitment began on 7th August 1914 the response was alarmingly poor when set against the War Minister's targets. It looked as if the earlier 'patriotism' on display, had, like the August bank holiday ice cream, begun melting away.

The small British Expeditionary Force, already crossing the Channel to dig itself into the unreliable soil of Northern France, was well short of the numbers needed even when volunteer part-time territorial units were added to their ranks. Uncharacteristically, the normally emphatic and self-assured Kitchener – a veteran of many past military campaigns – grew increasingly worried. He could envisage that come Christmas the bells ringing in his mind would have more to do with manpower shortages than anything connected to the festive season. How was he to meet the challenge of a Germany capable of putting millions of well-armed conscripts on the battlegrounds unless he could boost the B.E.F. (already described by the Kaiser as 'contemptibly small') with tens of thousands of his own volunteer soldiers? Understandably, his ears flapped when Rawlinson arrived to brief him on the thinking that lay behind the PALS initiative.

In the last week of August, with Kitchener's approval, Rawlinson piloted the PALS idea in the City of London, targeting recruitment at clerks, bank employees and other white-collar workers whose jobs lay at the heart of London's financial district. If the response to his call for volunteers was anything to go by then the City's motto, 'Lord Direct Us', seemed for once entirely suited to the occasion. Over 1600 young hopefuls made their way to Throgmorton Street on the day the recruitment centre opened its doors for business. The battalion subsequently raised became known as the 'Stockbroker PALS', later the 10th (Service) Battalion of the Royal Fusiliers. In the eyes of one military historian at the time the Stockbroker PALS was the epitome of what the country needed in its time of crisis: they were he wrote, *'..a very good type of Londoner, and a very good type of colonial.'* This affirming view of the PALS together with its sweeping success amongst London's upwardly mobile, ignited Kitchener's enthusiasm and seemed like the answer to his khaki-coloured prayers. He ordered the PALS scheme to be rolled out immediately to all parts of the United Kingdom.

General Rawlinson however, had other business to transact on behalf of the military, so the job of growing his brainchild was soon passed to others - civilians mostly, whose reputation for exercising influence over people and events within their localities was seen as being crucial. In Lancashire this meant the job fell to Lord Derby. As he stood in his room at the House of Lords, thumbs hooked in his waistcoat, Derby must have pondered deeply on the responsibility that now rested on his broad, sloping shoulders. Brought to his door was the task of putting up the bulk of men from Lancashire needed to win a war: and Lancashire wasn't London, so repeating the success of the Stockbrokers PALS was far from being guaranteed. Kitchener apart, Derby's close friends in the military, including Sir Douglas Haig, would also be relying heavily on the efforts of people like himself to provide the required number of recruits, without which their hands would be tied and all sorts of accusations would begin to fly. If he failed to deliver, Derby knew that his reputation would disappear faster than a rat down a battlefield drain.

Almost immediately, however, a way of getting the PALS scheme to stick suggested itself. As a Lancashire man Derby knew only too well the rivalries that existed between people belonging to the two great cities of Manchester and Liverpool. They went back a long way, certainly to the time when Manchester's famed ship canal opened and, almost at a stroke, threatened to put Liverpool's supremacy in docks and distribution into the doldrums. By the time of the First World War wounded feelings over this should have healed: but they hadn't, and the animosities between citizens of both cities continued to surface from time to time as Lord Derby was well aware. If he might just blow on the flames a little, make use of what was described as the *'uncompromising competition'* between the two cities then his stewardship of the PALS initiative could possibly get off to a flying start and become a model that the rest of the country would be happy to copy.

On August 27th 1914, posters promoting PALS enlistment began appearing all over Liverpool – a city where Lord Derby was the mayor. The local newspapers joined in, carrying adverts appealing for the voluntary enlistment of men '...*such as clerks and those engaged in commercial business*' much as Rawlinson had done in the City of London a few weeks earlier. As expected, news of this wasn't slow in getting through to Manchester.

The following day a group of businessmen, most of them proprietors and senior directors of companies in the textiles industry met in Manchester Town Hall to consider their response. The outcome surprised no one. If Liverpool could raise a local battalion of volunteers, then Manchester was more than capable of doing likewise: indeed, they said, we can do more! A resolution was passed calling for the raising of the first PALS unit from those employed in white-collar jobs in the city's warehouses and commercial businesses, giving it the title of the Clerks & Warehouseman's Battalion. Fairly soon, this being something of a mouthful, it gave way to the slicker sounding '1st City PALS.'

On Monday, August 31st, Manchester's Lord Mayor, Daniel McCabe, with the backing of major businesses like Tootal Broadhurst and The Fine Cotton Spinners & Doublers Association, made an appeal for men to volunteer giving in return what was considered extremely generous terms of engagement. The primary features of the offer were designed to ensure they attracted maximum interest from those seen by the recruiters as the main targets. In return for signing-up voluntarily for the First World War, a man could expect to receive the following:

- *Four weeks pay from the date he left his company to join the armed services.*
- *His job back after the war.*
- *Half pay for a married soldier during his absence, paid to his wife.*
- *Special arrangements for those single men with dependent families.*

In what appeared at first glance to be an inversion of the usual hierarchy of rewards, the offer only applied to men enlisting in the ranks. Officer material, drawn from the public schools and universities, were not included, and neither were those in the higher professions. You didn't have to be particularly quick-witted to spot the rationale involved: the aim of the proposal was to recruit from the many, not the few. The carrot was being dangled not in front of the thoroughbreds but relatively speaking...the workhorses.

Other conditions written into the deal were also intriguing. *'Should the government decide on compulsory training later,'* it stated, *'the offer will not apply to those affected by such compulsion.'* If this wasn't a strong hint that conscription was already figuring in the minds of some people, then the perspicacity of pundits at the time must have been at an all-time low and how did it sit alongside the oft-stated belief that hostilities would be over by Christmas? Had the Town Hall conference of business oligarchs and local dignitaries understood that compulsion would become increasingly necessary as the war went on and casualties mounted? Did they know something the rest didn't – that this was going to be a long war and one that would ultimately require the force of law to get the generals the army they wanted?

Whatever doubts were entertained it soon became obvious the PALS appeal was a runaway success. Recruiting centres were so choked with young, middle-class men seeking to volunteer they couldn't cope, and new ones had to be brought into operation. In the opinion of the Manchester Evening News the quality of the men putting themselves forward were *'...the type which one sees on Saturday mornings in winter carrying lacrosse *and football bags – clean limbed and strong young fellows whom the recruiting officer eyes in vain in peace times...*' The queues grew by the hour and as pictures at the time showed, bowler hats and straw boaters were as conspicuous as cloth caps were by their absence.

Companies too were rushing in with offers of financial assistance. From the boardrooms of the biggest firms to the drawing rooms of wealthy individuals, cash to clothe, feed and equip the PALS poured in. The Manchester Gas Company, having recently rejected a wage increase for its employees, found £7,000 in a 'reserve fund' (around three-quarters of a million pounds in today's money), and handed it over to the raising committee. Other city based companies and merchant houses weighed in with more modest amounts, which nonetheless helped swell the funds and meet the financial targets set by the Town Hall recruiters. Such was the success of the appeal, Manchester quickly decided to extend it and form several more PALS battalions. Six weeks after war had been declared recruitment of the 4th City PALS...destined to be Sonny Boothroyd's battalion...had been completed, and plans were in hand to raise several more. The duplicity that Lord Derby had used to kick-start the entire scheme in Lancashire was now forgotten in the praise that descended on him from all quarters. It seemed he had no further cause to fret.

Among those who had been quick to unlock their purses and donate to the PALS appeal, was a family who owned a chain of retail outlets that stretched from their base in Manchester to towns in Merseyside and beyond. They were called Seymour Mead and they showed no hesitation in granting £1,000 to the raising committee - around £125,000 in today's money. As well as rubbing shoulders on a regular basis with Lancashire's business oligarchy, Seymour Mead also had connections with the military-one of them, A. Seymour Mead, being captain of an infantry unit within the Manchester Regiment. When war was declared, in common with other city-based companies, Seymour Mead took a lead in encouraging their employees to volunteer for enlistment. Before the war ended 363 of them had joined up.

As they counted out the banknotes, Seymour Mead might well have reflected, however briefly, on the consequences of having so many employees absent on war duty. There was consolation in the thought that the 'sacrifice' the firm was making was unlikely to harm their reputation because Seymour Mead was in the grocery trade, one of several multiple-chains operating in a market that had become progressively more cut-throat and competitive as time went on. It was a sector that included amongst others the ubiquitous Maypole Dairies, and Lipton's which had already made a multimillionaire of its owner, the 'tea-baron', Sir Thomas Lipton.

Although Seymour Mead was far from being a major player in the grocery trade, their empire was still growing and connections with the military and those dominating the commercial life of Manchester had a value far outweighing its current size. Anyway, suffering a loss of staff was something all corporate contributors to the PALS appeal would have to endure in the circumstances. So Seymour Mead, whose name adorned their shop-fronts and would make its way eventually into the Manchester Regiment's roll of honour, envisaged little in the way of disadvantage resulting from the form of 'pay-patriotism' they so generously displayed.

As it turned out, of course, they didn't prove to be quite as adroit as they imagined. The arrival of food rationing three years into the war would begin starving grocery stores of their core business, and beyond that the real threat of famine in Britain due to a German naval blockade of British ports was to force all the high-street multiples to curtail their opening hours. Rationing and restricted-hours of course, had obvious knock-on effects on the firm's profits. None of this was within the circumference of most people's thoughts during those first heady days of cheering crowds and PALS recruitment. Only for a few volunteers perhaps did the connections between business and the military and between employers and enlistment lead to uneasy thoughts, although in the context of the monumental events taking place in the autumn of 1914 they were easy to stifle and dismiss.

Someone with a bit more time to contemplate such matters though was Sonny Boothroyd. Not yet old enough when war broke out to meet the minimum age for enlisting, he would have heard as time went on of the mounting casualty figures, of events such as the reversal at Mons where the regular army had been decimated, and how, as winter gave way to the Spring of 1915, there appeared to be little prospect of the war finishing soon.

What he really made of it all no one will ever know, and any fears he had of becoming a soldier he kept to himself. That was because Sonny too was an employee of Seymour Mead and would have to appear as loyal as any of the grocer's swelling contingent of shop assistants who were destined, so they'd been told, for better things....

Chapter 6

Though they donated handsomely in cash to the committee set up to raise the Manchester PALS, Sonny's employer, the grocery chain of Seymour Mead, was not invited to take a seat on it. Those tasked with the job of raising the volunteer regiments were men whose profile in the city's business sector was much greater than a grocer's, however successful. They were men drawn from Manchester's oligarchy, whose wealth derived mainly from the textile industry, and whose faces were as familiar within the boardrooms of major banks and finance houses as they were in the mills and factories where they employed tens of thousands of workers. Chief amongst them was the head of the Fine Cotton Spinners & Doublers Association, Vernon Bellhouse.

Under Bellhouse, the Fine Cotton Spinners & Doublers Association, had become a cartel – a form of business organisation fashioned from the merger of previously independent companies into a single corporate entity. Though they tacked the term 'Association' to the end of their title, the Fine Cotton Spinners were no Boy Scouts. Like all cartels they sought to protect themselves from competition by taking steps to eliminate it, thereby creating a monopoly. This was achieved largely through the relatively peaceful process of mergers and acquisitions, though anyone resisting the cartel's predatory advances could expect harsher treatment to follow. Engaging in price-cutting wars was a favourite way of bringing an obdurate independent to its knees – a kind of war of attrition fought without the need for trenches. Once victory over an independent company had been achieved prices were restored, usually at artificially high levels. Beyond that, cartels strove to monopolise the import and distribution of raw materials to dominate other industry sectors and to continue doing so through all fluctuations in the economic cycle. Between 1896 (the year of Sonny Boothroyd's birth) and the start of the 20th century, the number of cartels formed was at least equal in scale to anything that takes place in the world of big business today.

In the textile industry cartels and syndicates were forming faster than it took to spindle a hank of cotton. Two years before the formation of the Fine Cotton Spinners in 1898, the giant thread-making combine of J & P Coates had been established, and a year later another major cartel, the Calico Printers Association, came into being. More followed when firms in wool dying and bleaching became cartelised - enough evidence to show how the days of the independent producer were not just numbered, but effectively at an end.

There were, of course, problems to be overcome on the way to monopoly rule. Public concern was growing, and in the United States anti-trust laws had to be introduced to curb the excesses that made rich men richer and eliminated choice for the rest of the population. '*You can have any colour of automobile you want,*' Henry

Ford once said, *'providing it's black.'* In Britain there was the added complication of how to deal with the vanities and expectations of those who'd voted to have their long-established family firms disappear into the open jaws of a cartelised 'Association' or 'Trust.' In the case of the Calico Printers, for example, attempts to assuage everyone's ego resulted in the newly formed cartel ending up with a board of directors 84 members strong!

As head of the Fine Cotton Spinners, Vernon Bellhouse was a natural choice to lead the Manchester PALS raising committee. One of a family of mill owners and builders who'd already stamped their mark on Manchester, his powers of persuasion (if the Bellhouse family history is to be believed) were eminently suited to the task.

He was approached, we are told, somewhat casually by two other Lancashire mill owners towards the end of the 19th century with the interesting idea of forming what they described as 'an association of companies' engaged in the same line of business, in this case specialising in the spinning of raw cotton. It's a little difficult to accept this rather simplistic account of how one of the country's largest and most powerful cartels got underway: but this is how some historians have described it. It's like being asked to accept that those who invented the atom bomb just sort of run up against the idea one day when there was a bit of down time available in the physics laboratory.

Nonetheless, Vernon is said to have shown great interest in the idea and immediately set about lobbying other cotton spinners in Lancashire, persuading many of them eventually to sign up for the plan. As if to set an example he soon wrapped-up his own family business, selling it to the cartel and becoming the Fine Cotton Spinners & Doublers first executive director. With its heavy bank borrowings and robust capitalisation the Fine Cotton Spinners rapidly became the biggest firm of spinners and doublers in the world, at one point claiming to have over five million spindles at its disposal.

Bellhouse's success in forming the cartel enriched him personally and granted him the status of oligarch, a fact that wasn't expected to be overlooked when appointing him to a key role on the PALS raising committee. On the off-chance that Vernon might welcome additional support from like-minded associates, seated alongside him on the committee was another much approved nominee, A. Herbert Dixon, who just happened to be one of the two mill owners that 18 years previously had spun Bellhouse the idea of setting up a cotton cartel in the first place.

Also at the Town Hall table sat other men of substance, people who owned equally large portions of Lancashire's textile industry. They were mostly manufacturers, the producers of finished goods made from the cotton supplied at prices set by the likes of Bellhouse and Dixon through the Fine Cotton Spinners cartel. Stormy though the relationships between them must have been in the cutthroat world of commerce, wounds were bandaged tightly enough to allow the PALS appeal to be expedited at great speed.

Helping out in this respect was Edward. M. Philips, another PALS raising committee man whose family business, making woven garments and hats, could be traced back to the middle of the eighteenth-century. At the outbreak of the First World War his company, J & N Philips was a force to be reckoned with in both manufacture and merchandising with outlets in

Manchester and London. His most illustrious family member was Mark Philips, who became Manchester's first M.P. after the Reform Act of 1832 and who'd lived in some splendour on an estate set within the city boundaries at the time. The year after the First World War started J & N Philips became a private limited company, and as an indication of how little some people's fortunes suffered in the war, opted to float itself on the Stock Exchange in 1919. In World War Two part of the firm's premises in Manchester was used as a centre for censoring mail sent to their families by British soldiers serving overseas.

The dominant cohort within the PALS raising committee however, was unquestionably the men from Tootal Broadhurst, a company remembered by older generations today as the makers of wrinkle-free shirts. Though they were later to be swallowed up by a rival conglomerate, Tootal Broadhurst in its time was an outstanding example of an employer's combine – in this case, a company structured to carry out all the stages of manufacturing from processing the yarn to selling the finished item directly to shoppers through a string of retail outlets. The success of this 'vertical combine' for generating profits went far in justifying the cost of constructing the Tootal Building in Manchester's Oxford Street in 1898, complete with Corinthian columns and other features that owed their derivation to classical Greek architecture. When Tootal's finally folded, it was only natural you might think that such an imposing edifice should become the property of the Bank of England.

The man solely responsible for engineering Tootal's success (from spinning mill to shop shelve, as the company liked to put it) also sat on the PALS raising committee alongside his business partner, E. Tootal Broadhurst himself. He was Kenneth Lee, known only marginally better for his talent in developing vertical combines as for what a future acquaintance described as his '...*deliberation of speech, saved from being ponderous only by the shortness of his sentences and the sparseness of his words.*'

If Lee exercised the upmost economy with the spoken word, no such hindrance was evident in his unfeigned enthusiasm for making money, which allowed his father, a founding partner of Tootal's, the freedom to set about making himself a senior member of the Manchester business elite. At no little benefit to his son's future prosperity, Lee Snr. became a director of the Manchester & Salford Bank and for a time head of the city's Chamber of Commerce: and as the long history of the association between business interests and politics amply demonstrates, he also entered the House of Commons as the Member of Parliament for Southampton.

Appropriately, in view of Kenneth's appointment to the PALS raising committee, the Lee family had past connections with the Manchester Regiment. General Noel Lee who worked in the management of Tootal's whilst maintaining a close relationship with the military became the first territorial soldier ever to be made a brigadier – an accomplishment not guaranteed to set the pulses of most people racing, but which Kenneth was sometimes moved to mention. He on the other hand preferred his battles being confined to the boardroom, taking on the duties of company secretary then ultimately Chairman of Tootal Broadhurst Lee. In later years Lee was knighted largely because of his work for various government bodies, and during the Second World War was appointed Head of the Broadcasting Division in the Ministry of Information. Much in the same way as 'Association' was an attempt to veil the deeper workings of a cartel 'Information' in this context was a flimsy cover to what we now understand as propaganda. In his post with the Ministry of Information, Kenneth Lee enjoyed a close working relationship with the BBC.

Completing the cohort of businessmen who constituted the majority on the raising committee was Arthur Taylor about whom less is known, unless you take into account his habit of visiting the PALS at their training camps in the city, looking thin and slightly downcast as he traversed the muddy acres of Manchester's public parks in his beige suit and soft hat. It's likely he too had connections with the textile industry, but unlike the others his achievements in that respect failed to outlive him or suggest anything worthy of recording for posterity. Perhaps it was an attempt to put this to rights that encouraged Dixon to put himself within camera range when the press came to see the PALS being put through their paces.

Less anonymous however, though some would say not by much, were two other PALS raising committee members, the Lord Mayor of Manchester, Daniel McCabe and the committee's secretary, Arthur. E. Piggot. McCabe had been a local councillor in Manchester for almost 15 years before becoming its chief officer at the outbreak of the First World War. He was of Irish descent and something of a compromise candidate for Mayor in a city whose Irish population had risen to 15 per cent of the total following the great famine that had driven them from their homeland. Home rule for Ireland had been a key issue for government in the run up to the First World War, and divisions had emerged within Manchester's Irish community between those seeking devolution for the old country and others who demanded complete independence. Ireland at the time was Britain's oldest colony and frequently in a state of insurrection.

Now, with the arrival of the First World War, Ireland took on greater significance despite government plans to put it on the back-burner for the duration. Volunteer soldiers from both sides of the divide, Protestant and Catholic, were needed in the British army in the same way as men from other parts of the British Empire. To assuage the Protestants moves towards Home Rule were to be suspended: to encourage Catholics to come forward their church declared its support for the war arguing that the difficulties of a single country, Ireland, were insignificant against the threat posed to the entire world by German expansionism. It was time, according to the Roman Catholic Church, to bury old enmities and join together in defeating the danger that threatened everyone's door.

Out of this shifting paradigm of political compromise emerged the compromise candidate himself, Daniel McCabe – the man who was neither Sinn Fein nor overtly pro-British, and who might just be the fellow to hold both sides in balance long enough to see them all in khaki. Who can doubt that McCabe was handed the mayoral chain not through being seen as the equivalent in status to his counterpart in Liverpool, Lord Derby, but because he looked like the obvious figure to quell any prospect of the Irish in Manchester actively supporting a rebellion in Ireland at a time when Britain's attention was directed elsewhere.

Once appointed McCabe threw himself with vigour into the work of the PALS raising committee, issuing appeals for money and urging employers to prepare the way for their worker's *'voluntary enlistment.'* He was also party to drafting billboard and newspaper advertising in support of recruitment, including one directed at the partners of eligible men that asked, *'Will Manchester's womenfolk hold them back at this critical hour...the hour when the fighting man is the vital need?'*

Soon he'd be photographed taking the salute as the first Manchester PALS battalions marched off to embarkation for the Western Front. In his robes of office, complete with tricorn hat and gold chain, McCabe's short and rather corpulent figure stood out against the columns of eager young men in their spotless new uniforms and shiny boots. As often as not it rained on such occasions, but nothing could dampen the Lord Mayor's enthusiasm for his work...unless, of course, he was reminded of an appeal to raise a battalion from the ranks of his own council workers, something that had consistently failed to attract the requisite number of volunteers. Conscription was to loom before the Lord Mayor's efforts to form a battalion from Manchester's public servants was eventually achieved.

Seated a few places away from the Lord Mayor and thus closer to the elbow of Vernon Bellhouse, was the final member of Manchester's PALS raising committee, its secretary, Arthur E. Piggot. For once, here was an individual whose career had not been shaped by public office or involvement with the textiles sector but by an entirely different aspect of life, or as it was...death.

Piggot's business was funeral undertaking, and by the time of the First World War he'd shifted his locus of interest in the disposal of human remains away from burials to cremation. In land-owning Britain, problems were already being predicted for municipal authorities charged with providing cemeteries: so Piggot's advocacy of cremation had already attracted the interest of local councillors, city planners, and beyond that a distinguished group of supporters who included the British monarch himself. In time Piggot was to become convenor of the Federation of Cremation Authorities, and in a recent history of The Cremation Society of Great Britain he's described as a man '...*whose great work for cremation, not only in the district of Manchester but throughout the country, is familiar to all cremationists.*'

Whatever motivation Arthur Piggot had for putting himself forward for service on the PALS raising committee, and why the oligarchs welcomed his involvement can only be a matter for speculation. The temptation to link someone who knew death as it ordinarily took place with how it was likely to occur in the First World War, would be morbid and uncharitable. Yet more prescient minds at the time would no doubt be capable of envisaging the long casualty lists to come, to foresee the legions of maimed and wounded who'd return home with a shortened life expectancy so pushing up the mortality rates and putting even more pressure on the land available to bury them.

At any rate Piggot took his responsibilities seriously and settled to the many organisational tasks arising from that first Town Hall meeting in early September 1914, and those from the less momentous gatherings that followed. No doubt he fed back the healthy response of employers to the committee's appeal, kept the minutes, and oversaw how donations were being spent on training and equipping the PALS. Generally though that's where his contribution would end. He wouldn't enter much into the meat of the PALS raising committee's discussions, having neither the status nor latitude to do so. Nonetheless, his name appeared with the others on recruiting leaflets and advertisements, even if sometimes it looked a little like an afterthought added at the bottom of the sheet.

Such then were the league of gentlemen charged with the duty of turning the PALS idea into khaki-clad reality in Manchester. They were almost a vertical combination in themselves, six business oligarchs, assisted by a local luminary and a man whose main preoccupation was dealing with more economic ways of disposing with dead people. There can be few doubts they knew the First World War was going to be a lengthy affair, and the alacrity with which they sprang into action may even suggest they understood it as being necessary, and even welcomed it. The deal they drafted as an incentive to PALS enlistment clearly foreshadowed conscription: and its terms, couched in pay and job security, went straight to the factors most likely to have a potential recruit hesitating. Few things characterised the intention and composition of the Manchester PALS raising committee better than the deal they drafted and put in front of the city's young, middle-class men.

By any measure, those constituting Britain's PALS raising committees were regarded as clear-headed businessmen whose proprietorship of successful companies and cartels said all that needed to be said for their success in getting things done. If they didn't always recognise their children when Nanny brought them in from the nursery, the same wasn't true when they were considering the business opportunities they engaged with, and risk assessment became their sixth-sense. Yet here they were at the outset of a major war ostensibly gambling with their futures. On one hand they risked production losses by handing over employees to the military: on the other they risked seeing the seed corn of their future prosperity being thrown away on the unfruitful soil of distant battlefields. Some even came to losing a family member to the war, so in some ways what they did in pushing forward with raising the PALS battalion's, looks, at this distance, like a form of lunacy rather than how it was described at the time, as an expression of their patriotism.

As a firm with links to the military and Manchester's business world Sonny's employer, Seymour Mead, would have been well briefed as to what was afoot although their chief obligation, as the PALS raising committee saw it, was not just about donating cash but to round up as many employees as were eligible to wear the uniform and send them along to the recruiting centres. For them, and the 363 Mead 'volunteers' who put themselves forward for enlistment, the die was cast. A war was already underway and the call to arms and for men to do their patriotic duty was in full voice. When that was said and done what else remained except to salute the Mayor, march away from friends and family, and keep your fingers crossed that at no point would your nearest and dearest ever need to access the professional services such as those provided by the likes of Arthur E. Piggot.

Chapter 7

The letters posted by Sonny on the Western Front were addressed to his Mum, and found their way eventually to his family home in Manchester. The house, more roomy than the two-up, two-down dwellings that typified the city, was in Stanley Grove, Longsight, a wide thoroughfare carrying a double set of tramlines which swept in from the nearby junction with the Stockport Road.

The street owed its name to the existence of an old aristocratic family in Lancashire, Villiers-Stanley, whose pedigree in politics and the military stretched back over several centuries. The wealth amassed by the family from their extensive landholdings had enriched them to unprecedented levels which led ultimately to an earldom and a seat for each succeeding generation of Stanley's in the House of Lords. By the end of 1916, the midpoint in the First World War, the main beneficiary of the family fortune, Edward George Stanley, was made a cabinet minister by Lloyd George the man he'd earlier outraged by his opposition to social reform. Now he served in the wartime coalition government. Along with inheriting his family's wealth, Edward George also took his father's title, becoming Lord Derby (the 'Uncrowned King of Lancashire') who was given the task of spearheading the campaign to raise the Manchester PALS regiments for the First World War.

It is unlikely this meant much to the Boothroyds as they struggled with a more penurious existence at 3 Stanley Grove. Behind the sash-cord windows, their panes blacked out and taped against bomb blast, lived Sonny's parents and four siblings, in order of birth, Eva, Frank, Bertha and Alfred Boothroyd. Sonny filled the space between Frank and Bertha and had been born in March, 1896. Three years earlier another daughter, Minnie, had died in infancy.

Tending to the needs of a family that seemed to grow in neat, two-yearly increments was Sarah Boothroyd, Sonny's mother. Before being married she was preparing to become a schoolteacher: but a string of babies and several unplanned-for events ended that prospect. Her husband, Joseph, a storeman with a local textile distributor, was in most respects the stock father-figure of Victorian times – a man who automatically assumed the role of head of the household, but at the same time managing to stay inwardly remote from his children in a way emblematic of the mid-Victorian era he himself had been raised in.

Though Joseph Boothroyd strived to deliver what society asked of him – mainly the role of disciplinarian – like many other fathers he submitted eventually to failure. In small homes filled to the rafters with large families it was seldom possible to cause the degree of submissiveness demanded of children. So, in defeat he turned as many men did to even harsher ways of controlling his household: and when that also failed he took refuge in alcohol. It wasn't entirely his fault. Consuming alcohol was a common means of temporarily escaping the reality of being a serial failure, and the consequences physical abuse and the neglect of children became synonymous with drunkenness rather than with the impossible pressures exerted by society. The temperance movement, one of the enduring features of life up to the outbreak of the First World War, steadfastly refused to acknowledge any such connection.

Temperance never managed to attract Joseph Boothroyd's subscription however, and despite his position as a church officer he drank heavily for most of his life. He's remembered as suffering from 'fits', although uncharitably it has to said that blackouts were hardly unknown within the purview of Manchester's public houses at the time, especially on pay day. If he was frequently uncertain in his movements, his wife Sarah displayed the opposite tendency when she happened upon the bottles that Joseph often concealed within the confines of their home. With a great deal of sang-froid she'd march them directly to the outside privy and pour their contents straight down the throat of the lavatory bowl.

Sonny never mentioned his father in any of the letters he sent from the trenches. He sent love to his mother, to his brothers and sisters, passed on regards to his friends and acquaintances and members of their families: but never once did he refer to Joseph Snr. the father whose name he'd taken and which had been entered on his birth certificate. Perhaps this was due to no more than the accustomed animus between fathers and their teenage sons: or maybe Joseph's drinking impinged on Sonny's sensitivities more than it did on the other members of the

Boothroyd family. Alternatively, of course, there may well have been deeper feelings involved.

Joseph had never risen much above the level of an unskilled worker, leaving his job in the distribution sector to become a furnace stoker, then in middle age a cutter and grinder with an engineering firm. By becoming a shop assistant with a grocery chain Sonny had embarked from school on a much different type of occupation, one that was said to point towards a secure position in the retail sector or even having a business of his own. This in the view of his father might have looked like a son getting a bit above himself. Working class families were taught to see themselves as the *'pedestals on which great men stood'*, as necessary as those above them in the social hierarchy but still only supporting players in the *'great causes'* pursued by their betters. Indeed, this was precisely what was stated in a textbook used to teach children like Sonny at primary school. To see one's role in society as anything different was inconceivable whatever the apostles of *'self-improvement'* preached. In the eyes of men like Joseph Boothroyd any significant deviation from what was regarded as the norm was unacceptable Apart from anything else it carried the threat of undermining his position as head of the family, generating even more friction between himself and his children. No one will ever be able to say with certainty what built the barriers between Sonny and his father: but Sonny's motivation for omitting any reference to him in his letters was for once not due to military censorship. It was a rare case of the blue pencil not being required.

Eva Boothroyd though, Joseph and Sarah's first child, was proving to be a girl with many of the resilient qualities of her mother. She read and digested her brother's letters from the war, and often sent him a reply of her own along with the occasional photograph and a few small keepsakes. Eva was to be in her 30's before marrying, due no doubt to the First World War that had seen the end of so many men of marriageable age. In the interim she did a number of short-term, low-waged jobs and helped keep house at Stanley Grove. Her mother needed all the assistance she could muster, having other things to concern her besides a son risking death in the killing fields of Flanders. One of these was her oldest boy, Frank.

Frank Boothroyd, born two years before Sonny, had been the victim of a freak accident in childhood. Playing in the streets around his home he'd received a blow to the face from a horse belonging to a street vendor, and as a result suffered the loss of an eye. For obvious reasons Sarah Boothroyd was anxious about her son's future. His schooling had been disrupted and now the longer term prospect of finding work and earning a wage was proving difficult. As children do, however, Frank adjusted quickly to his disability and his workless state ended when in mid-life he became proprietor of a sweet shop just a few hundred yards away from his family's front door. When the First World War arrived he was deemed unfit for military service because of his visual impairment, which Frank must have seen as something of a mixed blessing the longer the conflict went on and the more the casualty rate multiplied. By all reports he is remembered as the most amusing member of the Boothroyd family, always joking, always making light of his disability and happy to be known as the 'Red One' because of his gingery hair.

If Frank Boothroyd was able to overcome the consequences of an enduring disability however, the same wasn't possible for the baby of the family, Bertha. From the moment she first drew breath in the late-summer of 1901, Bertha became what today is described as someone with learning difficulties – a condition probably caused by a bungled birth. At the time home births were the only option available to working class women like Sarah Boothroyd, and midwives were people whose skills in many instances fell below those required. Largely untrained, they learned on the job and had little in the way of recognised qualifications. They invariably lived near to where a confinement was due, or sometimes lived in the house of the expectant mother receiving board and lodging in lieu of a fee. Their reputation as midwives had more to do with their qualities as carers and organisers than with the expertise needed to carry out the safe birthing of a baby.

No one will ever know why Bertha Boothroyd sustained brain damage at birth, and it is possible Sarah like many mothers took some of the blame on her own shoulders. What can be said is that for the rest of her life Bertha had no choice but to stay within the fold of her family with just elementary forms of special schooling at her disposal and without hope of leading an independent life. She outlived both her parents, but is remembered as being silent and withdrawn. Her future nephews and nieces were always reminded to *'show Aunt Bertha some attention'* when they went on visits to Stanley Grove.

Although Bertha was to be the last of Sarah and Joseph's children (Sarah was 40 when she had her), there was another son whose birth came between hers and Sonny's. His name was Alfred and he was to hold a special place in Sonny's heart the way kid brothers often do. Alfred was a thin, quiet lad perfectly fit in mind and body which only increased Sonny's anxiety the closer Alfred came to being conscripted into the army. *'They'll be calling Alfred up shortly'* he said flatly, in a letter written as he waited for the Battle of Passchendaele to begin in July 1917. Although he avoided saying so directly to his brother, in the same letter regarding a mutual acquaintance who had just completed his military training, Sonny added *'I suppose he will be thinking of coming out here. Poor lad. I hope he has the best of luck, that's all I can say.'* In due course Alfred received his call-up papers as the trenches continued to demand their quotas of human flesh and blood. Before completing his training however, hostilities finally shuddered to a halt and the Armistice awaited. Alfred was to be spared what his brother had been unable to avoid.

Alfred outlived all of his family, remaining to the end of his days the rather subdued character he appeared to be in his youth. Perhaps in some ways he took after his older brother whose qualities of diligence and deference to others had made him ideal material for becoming a shop assistant. Alfred, however, chose to become a print operative, remained unmarried, and stayed almost to the end of his life alone at 3 Stanley Grove. When the debilities of age finally required him to move to a nursing home, he was to be seen on occasions returning to stand at the gate of his erstwhile family home gazing silently up at the windows.

The house must have held many memories for him, although when asked once about the First World War and his brother's murderous engagement with it, all he would say was 'Ah, that was a long time ago.' Sonny never failed to mention him in his letters, and the bond between them was never more evident than in the row of kisses added at the foot of the page. Throughout the years to follow Alfred was to keep close to hand the slim, mud-stained envelopes that dropped through the door of Stanley Grove, no doubt re-reading the letters they contained whenever his thoughts turned to the brother he'd known for such little time beyond childhood. Shortly after moving to the nursing home however, the house in Stanley Grove was broken into and the letters trampled under the boot of vandals. Only the intervention of a niece, Mildred (Boothroyd) Beech, rescued them for posterity.

In a way Alfred was yet another casualty of the First World War, one whose wounds remained hidden from view but whose pain was never fully in retreat. In some respects he may have suffered more than any of the other Boothroyd children, including elder brother Frank. Losing an eye it might be argued was insignificant when put alongside losing a favourite brother like Sonny.

Chapter 8

No sooner have they left the road and entered the first complex of communication trenches, than the men of Sonny's battalion are brought to a standstill. No one can say why they've been ordered to halt or how long the delay is likely to last - circumstances ideal for rumour to take over. In a war where names have become numbers and the monotony of mud is the landscape of a soldier's daily existence, the human imagination can often find its release only in rumour. Furthermore, rumour, which travels at the speed of a sniper's bullet, is capable of causing just as much alarm and anxiety.

The first rumour to reach Sonny's ears is that the much feared-for trench raid has taken place somewhere further up the column. This is soon quashed as wiser heads point to the amount of daylight remaining, and how the actual changeover at the frontline isn't scheduled for several hours yet. Gradually, more benign reasons for the delay begin circulating. Waiting for a consignment of trench stores to catch up is one: detailing men to clear an obstruction is another. The likeliest reason however, is that officers leading the way have their maps out and are at odds with the trench guides over the best way to continue.

The trenches here have been fought over so many times...have been shelled and bombed or simply disappeared in water...that it's often impossible to say if everyone's being marched in the right direction. New trenches have been dug, others cleared and extended: but many more have been left *un-cleaned* since Passchendaele, nothing more than mud traps that cleave still to the remains of dead soldiers belonging to both sides in the conflict. Given the option officers will choose to avoid such places, bypassing them in any way they can sometimes electing to use tracks out of the trenches that others have made in the foul, desolate landscape. The overall result is a labyrinth of interlocking and mostly flooded excavations and footways in which disorientation is common. Even the trench guides have been known to lose their way in the dwindling light.

Doing a turn of duty here is made even more difficult by the absence of the usual earth parapets, so that protection for anyone moving along the trenches has to be provided by anything that comes to hand. Concrete blocks, sheets of corrugated iron, bits stripped from abandoned equipment...anything that will stop an enemy bullet or deflect it from its target is utilised, even if the finished article looks disturbingly inadequate and far from what the military manuals recommend. In the narrow confines of these flimsy fortifications, Sonny's unit seek the best shelter available settling into a state of numbed acquiescence that has as much to do with the bleakness of their situation as the steadily dropping temperature. The frontline, they tell each other, will come soon enough.

For troops moving towards the primary danger zone the march forward, however long, seems to take no time at all. For those being relieved the same route back to relative safety will seem to take for ever. Whey-faced and bleary-eyed the men of the relieved regiment will look at times like so many sleepwalkers, dozing as horses do, in short intervals, standing up. Only the promise of a warm bath and more tranquil sleep will keep them going, although on this occasion so too will the chance of a belated Christmas dinner and the rare opportunity to relax at a Yuletide entertainment. What has been hailed as a cheerfully chaotic production put together and performed by the troops themselves is to be staged in one of the few buildings still standing at the rear. The show, already presented to great acclaim in other parts of Flanders, is to be repeated for men whose duties first time round had detained them elsewhere. On a broken tree stump by the side of the road, those of the relieved battalion (tonight it's the second battalion of the Wilts regiment) still able to focus their sight will spot a poster declaring the show to be a *'Hooge'* success!

For Sonny, however, the only available invitation to relax comes from a narrow projection in the trench wall, which he instantly commandeers before sitting down and looking glumly around him. On either side soldiers are divesting themselves of their heavier gear and arranging their rifles in vertical stacks between the slats of the duckboards. Though attempts have been made to dig the trench to army specifications, that being in a zigzag pattern meant to curtail bomb blast and enfilade fire, there are still too few corners to give everyone protection against the chill Flanders breeze. Like roosting birds, therefore, the men sit close to each other for warmth, or else burrow down into their greatcoats if they're still lucky enough to possess one whose skirts haven't already been hacked away to reduce the weight of mud and moisture that inevitably gathers there.

From the spare sandbags every infantryman is obliged to carry, an eclectic selection of items, not manifestly relevant to fighting a war, begin to appear. Newspapers recently delivered from home are creased open at the sports pages even though major sporting events in Britain like football matches have been suspended for the duration. Just as visible are much-thumbed copies of pulp fiction and pin-up magazines, which in the French editions show girls smiling seductively as they daringly display their ankles. Opposite Sonny a man bends his head over a letter which he reads over several times, silently mouthing the words in a way he will doubtless do umpteen-times again before a fresh one arrives in the mail.

Mostly though, what emerge from pockets and haversacks are the remains of food parcels sent from home. *'I received your parcel which I was very glad of,'* Sonny had written to his mother on several occasions. *'It's a treat to come out of the line and have a parcel waiting for you.'* Chocolate bars and boiled sweets, broken biscuits and bits of cake, tinned sardines and wedges of mouldy cheese all make brief appearances before being rapidly devoured. Comfort eating on the Western Front makes few concessions to how fit something is for swallowing, and soldiers eat with a sense of purpose rather than relish knowing that these remaining scraps…fastidiously hoarded and seldom shared…might be the last real sustenance to reach their stomachs over the next forty-eight hours. In the intervals between chewing almost everyone smokes, lighting their cigarettes from those already burning around them and hiding the glowing tip within a cupped fist. Shortly, even this small pleasure will be forbidden as darkness falls and the frontline approaches. Everything is rationed here, including light however feeble, and only the trench guides with their torches at the head of the column are given any leeway.

Suddenly though, within earshot of Sonny, a soldier unaccountably breaks into song before being hissed back into silence by those around him. This time rumour suggests the man is suffering from the delayed effects of *'shell-shock'*, although a more-likely explanation is that he's been saving his rum ration for this tour of the frontline – a plan now punctured by plummeting temperatures and the man's desire to start feeling its inebriating effects sooner. The soldiers gathered near the boozy balladeer look startled at first, then break up in silent mirth. The incident has helped ease the tension if only for a few moments and as the command to resume marching passes down the line, the men of the 19th battalion struggle to their feet still grinning.

Sonny levers himself upright and retrieves his rifle. He yawns and stretches, waiting while the others reinstate around their bodies all the equipment a frontline soldier is required to carry – a personal cargo of tools, ammunition and stores weighing more than fifty pounds. As he begins moving stiffly along the greasy duckboards, he finds the song of the errant soldier has stuck in his head where it replays endlessly like a demented audio-tape. He'd recognised the song even if its full rendition had been quickly snuffed-out. It's one that's been sweeping the Western Front for many weeks now, and its lyrics are neither difficult to remember nor easily forgotten. Sonny can't be sure of the tune, but under his breath he hums a reasonable attempt at how it goes.

> *'If you want the old battalion, I know where they are,*
> *I know where they are, I know where they are.*
> *If you want the old battalion, I know where they are,*
> *They're hanging on the old barbed wire.'*

Though wholly appropriate to what he's had to endure in the run-up to this the fourth Christmas of the war, the words are far from being festive or reassuring. However, for a while at least it takes Sonny's mind away from what might lie ahead in the hours yet to come.

Chapter 9

The dark vestments of the First World War were soon trailing their bloodied skirts along the streets of most towns and cities in the land, casting a shadow which left whole communities fearing the worst. Hopes for the survival of a loved one on the battlefields hung on very slender threads. When the length of the casualty lists grew to become an embarrassment for the government, they stopped releasing them to the national newspapers and the press published only those in the officer class who'd fallen. The effect was to increase the uncertainty and tension for families with soldiers serving in the ranks. They could only watch for the postman and hope that what he pushed through their door didn't include anything more than the familiar selection of mail.

Arguably, those who were returned wounded from the battlefields and designated unfit to ever fight again were among the more fortunate casualties. There were many thousands of them. Eight thousand men would return eventually with one or both arms missing, and upwards of 80,000 with other serious limb damage. A further 10,000 men would endure permanent eyesight problems caused by gas, many of them already completely blind:

and 15,000 would suffer hearing impairment, deafened by exploding shells and the effects of heavy artillery weapons being fired around them. Most common of all though were head injuries and diseases such as tuberculosis, bronchitis, rheumatism and heart disorders caused by excessive labour in appalling conditions. An uncountable number of victims were obliged to carry around metal plates in their skulls for the rest of their days. Added to the physical damage of course, was mental illness, *'shell shock'* and other neurasthenia that frequently led to paranoia and the inability to think and act in rational ways.

The wounded were usually returned to their native shores late at night so their grotesque injuries would not be seen by too many people. It was also a time when the daily newspapers had been put to bed, pre-empting any likelihood of the press giving such events anything but minimal coverage. Meeting them at the English ports were posses of medical personnel and a few be-hatted women serving tea, handing out Woodbines and offering a few words of comfort and consolation. From their pallets and makeshift stretchers the sick, the traumatised and those clinging to the last vestiges of life watched uncomprehendingly: many understood as little about where they were or how they'd got there, as to where they were being taken next.

Their main destination of course, was hospital: a journey that seemed to take for ever, first by train from the ferry ports then onward by road. In Manchester, Eva Boothroyd and her mother would walk the short distance from their home to join the crowds lining the junction of Stanley Grove with the Stockport Road waiting for the war wounded to go past. Somewhere near, Frank and a few of his acquaintances would also be present although Alfred would have been left at home with instructions to look after his sister Bertha. On Sundays, without church bells, a more joyless medley of sound would echo around the Longsight area – the banshee wail of ambulances.

Ambulances carrying wounded soldiers were often no more than requisitioned vans bearing the familiar red crosses. In Manchester they came in a long convoy from the city's main railway terminus. They were headed for hospitals in Cheshire and the arrow-straight Stockport Road offered the speediest route. Inside, their cargoes of injured men held on as best they could while the ambulances bumped and ground their way over the rough cobbles. More than a few failed to survive the journey: having defied death on the battlefields and the sea passage home, they were to be entered in hospital records as D.O.A. – Dead on Arrival.

On their side of the road Sarah Boothroyd and her daughter would stand close together clutching each other's sleeve, maybe linking arms with a neighbour, absorbing each other's shivers, sharing each other's dread. At different places in the crowd people waved flags or got ready to shout an encouraging word. As the grim realities of war came swaying down the Stockport Road however, enthusiasm waned and any outward signs of patriotic fever rapidly cooled to the silent sweat of trepidation and fear. Some people wept, some bent their heads as if in prayer. An elderly man, probably an old soldier himself, saluted as the first ambulance skidded by within a few feet of his raised elbow. Mostly though, the crowd looked on in silence broken only at intervals by a weak spattering of applause and some half-hearted efforts at raising a cheer. Some hoped that inside the makeshift ambulances lay one of their own. It would be some measure of relief knowing that someone dear to you was at last free of Flanders: even if mutilated and disfigured, at least he would be home and within reach of those who cared for him and care would reach beyond immediate medical support and the victim's family. That in many ways was what community was about.

At the time of the First World War, Manchester, like all industrial towns and cities in Britain was a place of close communities that meant something to those who were a part of them. Located within walking distance of the mills and factories that provided them with work, the narrow streets of back-to-back houses gave an identity, as well as shelter, to the vast majority of the city's population. They were not easy places in which to live and were forever blighted with problems that ranged from poverty and overcrowding, to alcohol abuse and high rates of infant mortality. Yet there was a strong attachment to locality and people born and raised in places such as Longsight grew a strong allegiance to them. *'What street are you from?'* was usually the next question after asking someone what they were called.

People met and married in their communities, had their kids there, and died without having moved more than a few streets away from their parents or the house where they themselves had been born. Only in extenuating circumstances, like doing a moonlight flit to avoid the rent man, did people ever move right away for any appreciable amount of time. If you were ever overtaken by an urge to travel and couldn't wait for the annual works outing, you went for a ramble round the neighbourhood or took a tuppenny tram ticket to where you wanted to go - usually window shopping in the city centre. A night-out would normally be enjoyed at one of the variety theatres dotted around the town - posher folk and people like the PALS parents in the back stalls and second circle, the working class in the gallery which had the worst views. In keeping with the times many places of entertainment including the growing chain of cinemas, had the word *'Empire'* or *'King's'* in their title. In later times, entertainment was manufactured from these working class communities – stage plays, soaps and T.V. shows *about* them as well as for them. However, the ghosts of the royal imperial past continued to haunt the naming of such productions, *'Coronation'* Street being just one example.

    The Boothroyds took their place in this jigsaw of totally urbanised communities that constituted the city of Manchester, communities that were predicated on the socialisation of work in manufacture and mass production which in turn grew *'socialised'* neighbourhoods. They were places where friendly societies, trade union branches, voluntary clubs and penny-insurance schemes were commonplace. Most of all though, the *sense* of community drew its strength from the recognition that just about everyone around you faced the same daily struggles for survival, and that no one was any more than a few factory shifts away from possessing nothing. Living close to the edges of destitution might not be seen as the best way of building strong communities: but that's precisely what existed, and there was always someone within reach when you most needed them. When someone from your community died, more than his immediate family experienced grief. The sense of loss was shared and how could it not? The footfall of someone you'd watched grow from a baby to infancy then into adulthood would be heard no more......

As the Boothroyd family grew or Sonny's father changed jobs, so they moved around the area of South Manchester in search of a bigger house:...first from the district of West Gorton to Gorton proper, then from Gorton to Longsight and 3 Stanley Grove. None of their homes were much outside a short tram journey of each other and all had piped water, basic sanitation and a front door that opened directly on to a paved street. Sometimes there was a miniscule front yard that yielded-up a scrawny shrub or two: but never what you would call a garden. The prevailing wind blew the filth and fumes of industry away from the western parts of Manchester where the better-off lived, and dropped it on to the homes of those whose work had caused the pollution to rise up the factory chimneys in the first place. In this respect the Boothroyds home town was no different from any other whose fortunes were made from the smokestack industries. The wealthier members of society lived in the West End: most other people had to make do with what was available elsewhere, usually in the East.

The average rent for a two-up, two-down, back-to-back house was around 5/6d a week paid to the agent of a private landlord. It represented 15 per cent of a skilled man's wage although rent increases in the decade before the First World War increased along with the general increase in prices. Meanwhile, wages in the same period remained static. For the workless, the old, the sick, the disabled...indeed anyone facing the threat of destitution and the workhouse, the streets of red-brick terraces often hid another evil that beset local communities – sweatshops.

Employers seeking to avoid the cost of having premises and paying the going rate for certain types of work, kept themselves outside the laws on health and safety by engaging vulnerable people to make products in their own homes. Making boxes and containers was a typical example of sweated labour, as was tailoring and activities such as button carding and bristle sorting. Even chain-making for a time was done in people's back rooms. Frequently whole families were involved in sweated labour, paid by the piece and not on a daily or hourly rate. A shilling per gross was the price paid for box-making, but only if you supplied your own glue. If necessary your children missed school to achieve the targets set by the employer.

Inside Number 3 Stanley Grove, Sarah Boothroyd also sweated…but over different sorts of labour. She sewed and darned her family's clothes, cooked and baked bread on the kitchen range, scrubbed and polished lino, cleaned windows, dusted furniture, carted coal and dumped ashes, all before turning to the endless cycle of washing and ironing that kept the Boothroyds looking as she wanted them to look. In between times she did the shopping taking care to balance a household budget constantly imperilled by the needs and wants of a growing family, not to say her husband's frequent binges.

In many ways the interior of Stanley Grove hadn't changed much since the turn of the century. Though the Edwardians had long since thrown their homes open to *'The Light!'* people like the Boothroyds were still to emerge from the penumbra of late-Victorian fashion. Velvet was still preferred to chintz, lino to rugs, patterned wallpaper to plain painted surfaces, curtains instead of blinds, and dark varnish took precedence over brightly coloured woodwork. Though they forever complained about it, fresh air came usually as draughts. Images which hung from the walls however, were becoming more popular. The Boothroyds had several pictures hanging in their front parlour, including a head-and-shoulders photograph of Sonny in his military uniform, the portrait of a youngster trying to appear serious and grown-up below the brim of his soft army hat. What was to happen to this picture became a spooky, if not entirely plausible legend, for some members of the Boothroyd family in years to come....

Out on the Stockport Road meanwhile the last ambulance has done a rough shimmy round the slow-moving traffic and disappeared, its red tail lamp flashing in the murky twilight. The crowd has already begun to disperse, quietly, solemnly, an un-reckonable feeling of guilt descending on them as if somehow they bore part of the blame for what had transpired in a war that now had no foreseeable end. Only the children present revert quickly to normality as kids do, mimicking the siren song of the ambulances until cuffed into silence by a grown-up.

Lying on the pavement, already accumulating damp and dirt is a cheap paper version of the Union flag that's been dropped and abandoned by someone in the crowd. A girl, who'll recall the scene half a century later, watches as her brother picks it up, folding it swiftly before stuffing it into his pocket. Tomorrow it will reappear as part of a street game...Britain against the Boche...a fight to the finish. No one will readily volunteer to be a German of course, although the bribe of a chewy caramel or piece of liquorice stick will go far in putting that to rights. No bets will be placed either on the outcome to the battle, that having been decided well in advance. When the enemy has been overcome the disintegrating flag will be flown briefly over his corpse before it's time for everyone to go home for their tea.

'Victor and Vanquished' could easily be the name given to such a game, although in the end nobody really wins, nobody really loses. Tommy and Fritz go back to being buddies again till the next time they have occasion to fall out. In many ways the streets are like the trenches, which in turn are like the factory production lines - long, narrow, populated by people dreaming of better times. Boys will become men, queuing for work, queuing for war. Many will die before their time without their families being given the reasons why, or who exactly was responsible for their death. Community pride will be called upon eventually to honour and remember them by erecting memorials and holding remembrance services. There will be a lot more graves to be dug: a lot more ambulances to come hurtling down the nations Stockport Road's. If only it was all just a game then things might be different...might even get better.

Chapter 10

Had Sonny been returned to Manchester for treatment to his trench-foot or a later shrapnel injury, he might have found himself spending time in the city's Moss Bridge Hospital. From the window of his ward however, he would have been able to catch sight of something disturbingly familiar: a First World War trench excavated in the hospital grounds. Built as a replica of those on the Western Front its sandbagged parapets, dugouts and duckboards offered guided tours to the public whose donations helped raise money for the care and treatment of the war-wounded. A group of disabled ex-servicemen led the tours, which finished by providing visitors with a can of tea brewed on a genuine British Tommy's cooker. The old soldiers also kept the place clean and disinfected, although the chance of any body-lice and other vermin giving visitors cause to itch was a remote prospect.

Visits to the real thing in France had been organised in the early stages of the war when Members of Parliament, munitions manufacturers and clergymen were among those invited to view how the troops lived and fought in their semi-subterranean habitats. However, the sites chosen were well outside the shell zones and like the

Moss Bridge replica saw plenty of advanced cleaning and tidying before the visitors arrived. However, there were still occasions when the distinguished guests got their clothes dirty and mud on their shoes clambering about in the rain. Nor were they invisible to the odd rat or two who'd chosen to ignore the military's injunction to bugger-off for a bit until the visit was over. As a result, many a dignitary dropping in on the Western Front opted for having the trench system explained to him without the need to leave a comfortable seat at Army Headquarters well behind the lines.

For the ordinary people of Manchester, desirous of getting a sense of what their loved ones were enduring in the war zones, a visit to Moss Bridge was the only option. Once the Lord Mayor and the gentlemen of the PALS raising committee had been and gone, it was time for the public to be admitted. No doubt members of the Boothroyd family, especially the older children Eva and Frank, would have been interested: and Sonny's kid brother Alfred would certainly have gone along with his chums, they being already within the shadow of conscription as 1917 progressed. To date two of Sonny's closest friends (referred to in his letters as Humph and Bill) were in training camp, and Alfred awaited his army medical and call-up papers. Understandably, Alfred would want to see what was in store for him, although he'd struggle at times to reconcile sanitised Moss Bridge with some of the descriptions of trench life given by his brother in his letters home. At the end of the tour when donations were sought, it's doubtful if Alfred and his companions would have been able to contribute much. Only those with the fobbed watches and rococo-style hats would have been able to manage more than the tram fare back to the city centre.

The city centre though, despite the constraints imposed on most people by the war, was a place for socialising, particularly on Saturday nights. After the shutters went up at Seymour Mead, Sonny would join his friends for a few hours of freedom which began at the foot of the Stockport Road. As they headed off towards the lights of central Manchester, the shop assistant would regale the others with stories of his working day behind the counter. There was always something to have a laugh about: or a moan. The old woman for example, reckoned to be filthy rich but nonetheless went shopping dressed in a tattered shawl which she used to conceal items that never made it through the cash register: and do you know what that stuffed-shirt of a store manager had ordered him to do about it? Why was Sonny always the one landed with the awkward and embarrassing tasks! As they made for the city centre Sonny's friends would weigh in with some equally loud and intemperate opinions of their own bosses.

Sometimes Alfred would tag along on these occasions, the other lads being closer in age to him than to Sonny: but Sonny was the leading spirit of the group, the shop assistant who'd bucked the trend of becoming an industrial worker and usually had some change rattling around in his pocket. At night, on the streets of their neighbourhood the older boy led the way, deferred to by his chums just as he in turn had to yield for much of his working day to the demands of Seymour Mead and its customers.

By this time Sonny was in his middle-teens and still growing, although he'd never be other than of slight-build and grow taller than around five-foot seven. He wore his fairish-hair cut short and his blue eyes were set in a complexion that was yet to show signs of facial hair. By nature he was quiet...shy almost except in the company of his friends, and as befitted a shop assistant he had learnt how to be deferential and dutiful, something his employer Seymour Mead insisted upon.

The boys he went around with all lived in streets next to Stanley Grove and had attended the same school. School was where they first began forming the bonds of lasting friendship although in other respects it was difficult to see how the new Edwardian era had changed much from what had existed in Victorian times. School was attuned more to preparing children for their pre-designated places in society, and anything beyond acquiring the basic skills of literacy and numeracy was looked on as something of a luxury. Featured prominently on a child's timetable were things like sorting beads before threading them on a string, or sewing simple designs on canvas squares. A great deal of emphasis was placed on getting children to sit still without talking, and in lessons they were often made to sit with their arms behind their back while teacher spoke. As a place for developing a child's latent abilities, school was a big let-down and as a consequence most children didn't exactly enjoy being there.

Class sizes were huge, accommodated in rooms that stepped incrementally to the rear and whose walls held little more than a few cases of botanical specimens and a map showing the extent of Britain's land grabbing successes around the world. A clock ticked the unbearably slow minutes away as children laboured at their writing and sums. Learning by rote was the standard approach to teaching – getting pupils to repeat endlessly the multiplication tables, or chant the values attached to coins of the realm.

'Twelve pennies equals one Shilling! Twenty Shillings equals one Pound!'

A pound incidentally was about as much as most of their fathers brought back from a week's work.

Each cast iron desk in the classroom was equipped with an inkwell and a wooden shafted pen whose unreliable nib would be forever spraying ink in all directions. Girls, therefore, stuck to the Victorian habit of wearing pinnys to keep their clothes clean, a sartorial regime their mothers, struggling with the laundry generated by a large family, had something to be grateful for. In Sarah Boothroyd's time there was no really effective remedy for dealing with ink and other indelible stains.

The Victorian intolerance towards children who were left-handed continued into Sonny Boothroyd's era. Rationalised because many jobs, such as menial office work, for example, were done sitting in rows, then left-handers would have a *'disrupting effect'* on those seated alongside. Consequently, schoolchildren often had their left hand tied to their side so obliging them to write with the other. Girls fared no better than boys in this respect... the argument in their case being that in domestic service (seen as the destination for most working class girls), cooking utensils were always positioned for being picked up by right-handed people. Left-handedness therefore, despite the gobbledegook and superstition accompanying it had more to do with work than with witches, and was seen as something to be drummed out of children at an early age. Various techniques were introduced with little success, while others were simply abandoned as being useless. Just to encourage compliance when all else failed, the cane was always visibly displayed at the front of the classroom.

Outside of school, children were tolerated in the growing number of public libraries appearing in the community. Children seeking admission though had first to hold out their hands for inspection. If not considered clean enough they were sent away to scrub them with carbolic soap before trying again. Having finally gained access they were made to sit on long, uncomfortable wooden benches overlooked by the gimlet eye of an attendant who's own achievements in school appeared to consist of learning to say, *'Be quiet!'* and *'No talking!'* in a loud voice. Discipline, in school as elsewhere, always counted as one of society's main priorities.

As they grew to an age where primary school was something to leave behind, Sonny and his friends looked increasingly towards getting work rather than continuing with their formal education. Legislation had ensured a 100 percent enrolment for primary schools: but that's where it ended. Just over 5 percent of children went to secondary school but the mass literacy that flowed from compulsory schooling created opportunities for others to profit. Publishers were especially keen to cash in with adventure stories for children which filled the pages of *The Boy's Own Paper, Pearson's Weekly* and other publications carrying tales of the straight-backed Puritanism that characterised the age. Alfred Harmsworth (later Lord Northcliffe) and his brother Harold (later Lord Rothermere), were just two of several press-owning oligarchs who were not inclined to sit with their hands tied to their sides when there was money to be made.

Northcliffe founded his first newspaper, *'Answers To Questions'* in 1894 targeting it at those he himself identified as having been *'taught to read but not to think.'* In the year Sonny Boothroyd was born, Northcliffe added to his growing number of titles by launching the *Daily Mail,* described by the then Prime Minister Lord Salisbury as *'a newspaper produced by office boys for office boys.'* Far from being offended at this apparent put-down, Northcliffe was only too pleased by the comment. That, he replied, was precisely the paper's strength! Filling the Mail with social tittle-tattle and interminable brain-numbing serialisations, he announced that the paper stood for *'the power, the supremacy, and the greatness of the British Empire.'* His connections with those in the political elite must surely have felt a little discomfited on hearing this view of their role in the world. Heavens above! The great British Empire reduced to the level of pulp fiction punctuated by pieces of gossip and idle chit-chat? Nonetheless, they didn't feel it necessary to stand in Harmsworth's way.

Early in the First World War, Harmsworth in a sudden rush of blood began attacking Lord Kitchener and the Prime Minister over a shortage of munitions needed at the Front. His newspapers lost 1.2 million sales as a result causing Harmsworth to rethink his approach to the issue. This he duly did softening his attacks until he'd regained the politician's favour. Lloyd George became his biggest fan thereafter, and in 1917 invited the press magnate to join the Cabinet. Harmsworth graciously declined. Instead, he was made Director of Propaganda for the remainder of the war.

Some of Harmsworth's publications no doubt, would be found blowing along the gutters of the Stockport Road on a Saturday night as Sonny and his chums went in search of amusement. Temperance, and later wartime restrictions, had the effect of emptying the pubs early, but the variety theatres only cascaded their audiences on to the pavement shortly before midnight. Mill girls, all toffed-up for a Saturday night on the town, would stream from halls like *'The Palace'* where tuppence had got them a seat in the gallery. It must have been tough on their nether regions sitting for so long on hard, cushionless seats: but what was a bit of discomfort when there was a good laugh to be had!

Doubtless, some of them would give more than a second glance in Sonny's direction as they made for the trams that would take them home. Even in the gaslight they would see him as a presentable lad...fair headed, clear eyed, unlike most of the boys they knew, his skin unblemished by the scarifying effects of factory work.

Sonny would flush slightly at their attentions, but his sidelong glances would reveal how the girls had taken to wearing their skirts above the ankle and often slit up the sides: a fashion sensitive to the growing utilitarian need of women for assistance when stepping up on public transport or riding a bicycle. Alone, the girls were as timid as mice: but in a group they were transformed, spontaneous, teasing, free with their language and their opinions of the boys grouped on the pavement. The boys on the other hand would scuff the ground with their toes, all previous banter now reduced to self-conscious mumblings. Sonny, being the eldest, would be only too aware of his feelings towards girls: but the yawning gender gap between himself and these precocious teenagers was as wide as the Stockport Road itself and what would Seymour Mead think of him seeing a mill girl outside of working hours? If shop assistants were encouraged to see themselves as being somewhat superior to factory hands, what view would his employer take of Sonny trading-downwards for a mill girl's affections? It was a tricky business this thing about girls: it wasn't just having the confidence to chat them up, it was making sure they were the right sort to chat up in first place!

When the girls disappear, the boys find their tongues again and cluster around Sonny eager to discuss them. Sonny, being older, is seen as a source of much-sought after information. After all doesn't he talk to females on a daily basis in his work at Seymour Mead's? The maid-servants, for example? He must know something of their secrets, surely! Sonny, however, is all for changing the subject. He knows about as much as any male does about women: even older men, married and with several children, will appear sometimes to have a more intimate knowledge of football than the opposite sex. So the shop assistant suggests going for an ice cream instead, or fish and chips, and then checking to see if that new cinema, the *'Queens'* is still open for business despite the lateness of the hour. Maybe, he thinks, Hollywood will reveal more about women than hanging out on the Stockport Road ever will....

Chapter 11

Sonny Boothroyd and the men of the Manchester Regiment are not the only things on the move this dark December day in Flanders. Other warm-blooded creatures are also astir - vermin mostly, like body lice and rats. It's a toss-up which of these two pestilential breeds soldiers hate most and they've taken to cursing both with equal vehemence. In a recent letter to his mother Sonny had added vermin to the vicissitudes of trench life by referring to every soldier's daily battle with a different sort of enemy

April 1917
Dear Mother
If this is what they call sunny France give me slutchy Manchester any day. There is only one thing that keeps us alive and that is the rats and lice. If it wasn't for them we should all snuff it.

Body lice are carried by just about every soldier on the Western Front. Ninety-eight in a hundred men are reckoned to provide hosts for the parasites. Unlike the troops however, lice find conditions in the trenches an ideal environment in which to prosper. Their numbers grow rapidly in conditions where men huddle close for warmth, living in the seams and fibres of their uniforms and nesting in the tangled forests of their body hair. Each female louse lays more than a dozen eggs a day, even more in times of the human stress that is only too prevalent on the Western Front. Dirty-white in colour, they grow to around three millimetres in length by feasting on a man's blood. They bite through to the blood supply, depositing an anticoagulant which afterwards leads to a maddening itch. After drinking their fill they withdraw, but only for as long as it takes for hunger to drive them out again in search of sustenance.

There is nothing at all anyone can do about them and body lice are no respecters of rank: officers are as plagued by them as the men they command. Before starting on today's march Sonny had run a lit candle along the seams of his clothes trying to burn them out. He'd also washed and scrubbed himself red at the baths - all to no avail. To put paid to the bloodsuckers for any appreciable amount of time, clothes require dry-cleaning or else laundered in hot soapy water but where in Flanders are such utilities to be found? Only at General Headquarters, the troops would say, where the top brass sit making their own plans for fetching out blood. Since that lies a good twenty miles behind where the trenches are, a soldier has no option but to continue cursing the brutes...and to go on scratching.

If body lice are a silent army of attackers, the same is no way true of the rats which roam the battlegrounds. Brown rats...black rats... they seldom appear much in any other colours. They forage in the discarded tins of bully beef soldiers sling over the trench walls, rattling them demonically as a prelude to the grisly night music that will follow. Besides feeding from the scraps of jettisoned food, rats invade the trenches and dugouts for tastier morsels or go in search of the sustenance provided by fresh corpses.

They invariably start by taking the eyes of a dead soldier, then burrow through his flanks looking for his liver. Once, on encountering a pile of slain soldiers while on patrol, a British infantryman recorded how he saw rats running from under their greatcoats. Enormous rats, he said, fattened beyond belief with human flesh. *'My heart pounded as we edged towards one of the bodies. His helmet had rolled off. The man displayed a grimacing face stripped of all flesh, the skull bare, the eyes devoured: and from his yawning mouth leapt a rat....'*

Rats grew, it was said, to the size of rabbits and the bigger they got the bolder they became. They would take the food from a sleeping man's pocket, and many a slumbering soldier was jolted awake by a rat sheltering in his blanket or crawling over his face. Because one breeding pair of rats could produce upwards of 800 offspring a year, the dugouts swarmed with them at several points in the season. Despite being bayoneted mercilessly in the trenches, it was an offence for a soldier to shoot at them. A waste of ammunition the army said... a waste of a bullet meant for the enemy. In the context of their multitudinous breeding, of course, it would also have been a waste of time. In a way, the rats might have been seen as an exemplar for the military's attitude to the slaughter of its own foot soldiers. Replacement drafts required? Righto! Coming up shortly!

The trench walls also gave sanctuary to other varieties of wildlife, marginally more-benign creatures like horned beetles and slugs, colonies of spiders, and insects that scuttled and leapt, slithered and slid especially when men digging and improving their fortifications disturbed them during the hibernation period. To show their disapproval, some of them often gave a nip in passing – a sting that hurt initially, then turned into another cause for scratching.

Out in the water-filled shell holes, however, the frogs have long deposited their spawn and gone silent. Films of ice form on the pools they once inhabited, in most ways useless now, stagnant and polluted by any number of poisons including the putrefying remains of soldiers and dead horses. Even the most ravenous rats might have to think twice before venturing into such places.

At a speed comparable to that of a trench snail, Sonny and his comrades now begin picking their way over the slippery duckboards, fearful no less of the distant chatter of machine-gun fire than of losing their footing and toppling over. It's beginning to grow quite dark now although a sailing moon promises to provide enough light to show the way forward. If any man has thoughts of the other warm-blooded creatures around him, they are by any demarcation short-lived and verging on the whimsical. Why, they might ask, does so much wildlife manage to survive where so many men don't? Within the narrow pre-programmed existence forced on them by nature, what enables vermin to endure the shelling and bombing, and especially the all-pervading effects of poisonous gas? The answer is something every stricken soldier would have given anything to know. The prick caused by a parasite after all, would be infinitely preferable to the hole made by the bullet which ended his life.

Chapter 12

Vermin of a more benevolent nature were on hand to greet Sonny when he arrived in Shropshire to begin his army training. Field mice scuttled around the billet he shared, and insects were not beyond delivering the odd bite: but their presence came low down on the list of things trainee-soldiers had to bother about as they took their next giant step in the direction of the battlefields. Other, more ominous matters, soon took precedence.

In several ways Shropshire was an appropriate place to train soldiers destined for the Western Front. Its flat northern plain where Sonny was drilled and paraded bore some resemblance to Flanders and the other combat zones where he'd spend his time on active duty. It also rained a lot in Shropshire, making mud. The area's economic history also provided parallels, the towns of Coalbrookdale and Ironbridge with their deposits of coal and metal ores having written themselves into the annals of Britain's Industrial Revolution in much the same way towns in Belgium had or for that matter, industrial Lancashire. Though he'd left *'slutchy'* Manchester behind, it wasn't always possible for Sonny to escape the evidences of what had made his native city one of the powerhouses of the world.

By volunteering for the First World War Sonny had signed-up to what soldiers called the P.B.I. – the Poor Bloody Infantry. They were the foot-soldiers of Kitchener's new army, men who'd be the first to go over the top in battle and the last, as they saw it, to garner any great credit for it. Once landed in France their hours of active duty would be spent mostly in holes of one sort or another - holes they themselves had made in the way of trenches and dugouts, holes gouged in the earth by enemy shells, holes that for many who survived the conflict would be forever remembered as the final resting places of their comrades. No less a part of this were the *'holes'* in Flanders that constituted the *'girdle of graves'* referred to by King George after the war was over.

Once in uniform, however, and in receipt of three hearty meals a day Sonny spent the next ten months in reasonable comfort and surrounded by more than a few familiar faces – other PALS who got a mention in his letters home:

No.3 Training Camp
Prees Heath, Salop
July 1915

Dear mother...just a line to let you know I am still alive and in the pink. Having a fine time here. I got the parcel you sent last week. Tell our Frank, Wallace Walker is here and Gosnell has gone to Salisbury again. There are some of them going to Blackpool for the winter in billets, but I don't know if we'll be going or not. I have no

*time now so I will write again. Hope you are all well...
Sonny.*

Before Manchester's raising committee had even begun drafting its PALS appeal in September 1914, the facilities for training army recruits had already been overwhelmed. So in the city just about every building capable of drilling volunteers was requisitioned. Church halls, school playgrounds, industrial sheds and city centre venues like the Free Trade Hall were all taken over and brought into service.

Some men were lucky to find accommodation with relatives near to their training ground, but thousands more remained in their own homes during the first phase of the war taking the tram to where they'd been ordered to report. By mid-September, as a result of the PALS appeal, recruitment rocketed and local parks, put at the disposal of the military by Mayor Daniel McCabe, grew acres of tented villages where men were put through their paces bereft as yet of uniforms and rifles, marching instead in their suits and brandishing sticks. Not that anyone grumbled much by all accounts. The new battalions, perceiving themselves as an elite force drawn from a better class of individual, mustered and marched, saluted and sang, and put themselves through everything their commanding officers demanded of them. In their very un-military apparel they might easily have been labelled the Bowler Hats & Boaters battalions.

Sonny's basic training began with *'hardening'* – the term describing the process of getting a recruit into the physical shape required for combat. Route marching was the principal tool for *'hardening'* and was also seen as a means of inculcating military discipline. Exhausting 20-

mile marches in full kit were regular occurrences and continued when the PALS arrived on the Western Front, leaving them on occasions barely able to carry out normal daily maintenance duties much less engage with the enemy. Alongside this went more specialist instruction for different units of the army: in Sonny's case learning the infantryman's skills in handling a rifle and using a bayonet.

The use of a bayonet in close combat figured in every infantryman's training despite evidence that the British army's version of the weapon was too long to be effective, and in the narrow confines of many trenches more of a hindrance than a help. The fact that the military establishment persevered with them is often taken as an example (like the belief in cavalry charges) of how ill-equipped mentally they were in understanding the new-technology of warfare – something that couldn't be said of the Germans. Wars we are told gives impetus to invention and innovation, although what they cost in human lives when they fail to live up to their promise is seldom referred to. In the First World War many soldiers resorted to manufacturing alternatives to the bayonet, producing knives and wooden clubs for use in close-combat situations. However, the army persisted in training men in the use of the bayonet, replacing gumption with gung-ho.

'During training,' one youthful volunteer recalled, *'I was aware only of the glamour of war. I prepared myself for it with enthusiasm and bayoneted and clubbed the stuffed sacks representing the enemy with a sort of exalted ferocity.'* Standing for the first time on the fire step of a battlefield trench, his elation remained undiminished. *'I remember saying to myself exultantly...*

You're in at last...The greatest thing that's ever happened!' Perhaps, in the light of what was to follow, an even greater thing happened in that he survived to remember his days spent bayoneting bags of sawdust at his training camp.

As the time for Sonny's shipment to the battlefront loomed ever closer, more ominously relevant routines began adding themselves to his training programme. Ways of surviving a gas attack made its appearance along with how to staunch the flow of a comrade's blood with the help of a few temporary field dressings. Included also were what was seen as the survival skills needed when slithering across no-man's land to set and repair the barbed-wire entanglements. Increasingly, however, lectures on taking orders and obeying them without question began embedding themselves in every recruit's preparation for war. Soldiers, almost without exception reacted by describing this as *'bull'* – nothing more than calculated attempts to stifle and suppress individual initiative. They were right of course, but their dismissive attitude couldn't conceal their status as victims of a paradox that had carried over from Victorian times: the appeal to individualism along with an unwavering obedience to higher authority.

This confusing hypothesis (one which surfaced again in the 1980s) had begun life in mid-Victorian times under the banner of *'self-improvement.'* Although it had provided a tool for boosting an individual's performance in the workplace, in one area at least it proved to be an anomaly verging on the absurd. That was in the military. Doing what you were told as against acting from personal belief or reasoned thought was seen as a key part of training a soldier for battle. The dichotomising of life into *'freethinking'* and *'obeisance'* didn't stand an earthly in the minds of the military top brass. Faced with any criticism the army simply dismissed it (as they continue to do today) by arguing that the military has to be *'pragmatic'* if it is to succeed. Suppose, for example, the officers of an army unit made a palpable mistake in planning an attack. Suppose everyone in the ranks could see it? The answer was to obey...to carry out the order and talk about it later. Trouble was, when later arrived you might well not be around for the debate.

However, despite all the *'bull'* and rigid rehearsals in training camp and on the muddy parks and playing fields at home, men continued to arrive on the Western Front unprepared for the reality they were about to face. As an infantry unit Sonny Boothroyd and his comrades had a major role to play in the strategy for winning the war. It was a strategy which held unswervingly to Douglas Haig's vision of first flattening the German lines with heavy artillery bombardments, then sending his foot soldiers over to make gaps in the barbed-wire so that the cavalry could burst through scattering the enemy to the four corners. It was a view of victory none of Haig's generals ever seriously challenged except with hindsight, and one which troops in their training camps were encouraged to see as the master plan for proving themselves the exclusive force they purported to be. Their first taste of the trenches...their first encounters with machine-gun fire and deadly shrapnel, would soon destroy this self-assurance for ever.

In the opinion of many historians Haig's myopia regarding machine-gun fire was one of his major handicaps. He clung to the belief we are told, that machine guns chattering out their icy messages of death were much over-rated – just a new-fangled piece of technology, insignificant as far as balancing the odds in favour of an Allied victory was concerned. He was even said to believe that the horses carrying his cherished cavalrymen were immune to machine-gun bullets, suggesting they had hides much like armour plating. Such reviews of Haig's thinking are not just difficult to comprehend: they are simply impossible to accept.

As a veteran commander of earlier wars Haig, like his boss Kitchener, could not have failed to appreciate the killing capacity of guns designed for rapid, concentrated fire. As far back as 1870 the British army had tested the Gatling gun, and 20 years later had adopted Hiram Maxim's machine-gun that could fire off 500 rounds a minute – the equivalent to upwards of a hundred rifles operating at once. By the time the First World War arrived Britain had its own Vickers machine gun, in addition to the Lewis gun, and if these were clearly fewer than what the military wanted they were still as familiar to them as the Lee Enfield rifle was to the infantry. In due course rapid fire armaments were also fixed to armoured carriers and aircraft. It was not possible for Haig to be unaware of this, so his '*blindness*' as historians describe it to the devastating effects of the machine-gun fails to be convincing. Other reasons more aligned to reality have to be sought.

It is more likely the field marshall had from the start decided that the numbers game was the one that mattered most. *'No amount of skill on the part of the higher commanders,'* he stated prior to the Somme, *'no training however good...no superiority of arms and ammunition... will enable victories to be won without the sacrifice of* men's lives. The nation must be prepared to see heavy casualty lists.'

From the beginning it is clear Haig's strategy greatly reduced itself to counting heads. The notion that he was consistently duped by his intelligence staff and senior officers over the havoc being wreaked by shelling and machine-gun fire in the combat zones, defies rational debate. Equally, the pundits view that he was below par intellectually, a blunderer whose pig-headedness and obduracy was the cause of the carnage gets us no closer to the truth of why he persisted in sending troops, chests expanded to the bullet, to their death for almost as long as the war lasted. In Haig's estimation, counting how many had been killed and how many left standing on each side was the deciding factor on who had won any particular battle.

Why this was the case lay in Haig's past as a general and in his experiences under Kitchener's command in other wars but to Sonny Boothroyd and his PALS none of this was other than a closed book as they slogged away on Shropshire's flat plain, digging dummy trenches and bayoneting 'Germans' made from potato sacks stuffed with sawdust and dried manure.

After a fortifying meal Sonny and his fellow-infantrymen would queue for an evening pass to the neighbouring towns, the war still distant, the bars and bright interiors of places such as Whitchurch much closer and seductive. Nice girls might still prefer sailors, but there were plenty more who were just as happy with boys wearing khaki. At the end of the night the revellers would return to their billets in less than strict marching formation, hopefully before the prescribed hour for lights-out and in search of their own beds. If time allowed they'd chat, play cards, sometimes scribble a short letter home usually addressed to their mothers. Among them were youths who'd lied about their age and whose recruiting officers had lied about their height or physical condition. Their employers, if they had one, would have known this but had demurred only briefly over their departure to the military. Tomorrow would bring more training, more *'bull'*, more being bawled at by the universally reviled drill sergeant. There would be time perhaps for a haircut, for getting something for those blisters, and working out when you'd next be up for a spot of home leave. They joked, squabbled and played pranks on each other in between presenting themselves for the endless round of fatigues and inspections demanded by their officers.

Seldom, if at all, did they fall to wondering about the one obvious gap in their training provision, or if they did then they didn't dwell on it for long. Never were they shown the procedure for burying a fallen comrade on the battlefield, although by this time – the spring of 1915 – news of the rising casualty figures was filtering back from the trenches. There again, there probably wasn't an awful lot to learn about a battlefield burial. It was: just another hole in the ground, this time with a different purpose in mind. The entrenching tool they were all obliged to carry was, after all, an implement that could be put to a variety of different uses.

Chapter 13

What Sonny Boothroyd experienced after reaching France in the spring of 1916 must have loosened the grin on his youthful face. He arrived from his Shropshire training camp amidst preparations for the Battle of the Somme, and found himself with barely three months in which to 'harden' his soldiering for what lay ahead. 'Hardening' came in the form of long and exhausting route marches, though even in the intervals between there was little opportunity for proper rest. He hauled trench supplies and munitions, helped in the building of a light railway, and was detailed to dig 'saps' – tunnels that ran from the British frontline under the German trenches which were then packed with explosives ready for detonation when the signal was given for the Somme to begin. If ever a lull in the daily round of digging and tunnelling looked likely, the army quickly filled it with battalion sports days: another way, as the military saw it, of maintaining discipline and aggression in soldiers until the time came for them to be summoned into action.

At least Sonny was in the company of familiar faces. He arrived with men he had trained with in Shropshire to be greeted by others who made up the 4th City PALS.

Some faces, of course, were no longer to be seen. These had belonged to men who'd made their mark on the First World War and then vanished, for ever. The previous January, so fierce had been the German bombardment north of the Somme where the Manchester PALS were in trenches, that the battalion had been unable to be relieved at the appointed time. Several of Sonny's 'familiar faces' had perished as a result. Then in May, 1916, fifty more were lost in the space of an hour when enemy guns opened up on units digging a new trench less than 200 yards from the German frontline. *'Gone West'* was how Sonny's comrades described them when he enquired of their whereabouts.

Towards the middle of June, 1916, the 4th City PALS were formally briefed that along with men from the Liverpool Regiment, they would be the first to go over the top at the Somme. This was received with no little enthusiasm amongst the fresh drafts of newly arrived volunteers according to some reports, although what they must have felt inwardly is usually ignored despite being obvious. Everyone knew a 'big push' was in the offing, a major offensive designed to rupture the enemy's line creating the breaches through which the cavalry would pour. After seemingly endless preparations for battle the prospect of engaging with the real thing was guaranteed to heighten the pulse rate of every freshly arrived volunteer. Practice now took on a different character. Fatigue seemed to evaporate. Even *'bull'* (the pep-talks delivered by senior officers) was listened to without the usual levels of scepticism. It was as if the dress rehearsal was coming to and end and the players waited with barely concealed excitement for the curtain to rise. Shortly before zero hour, Sonny attended a church service where the padre recalled how Christ himself had given up his life for others, and how Sonny and his fellow infantrymen were now being called upon to face a similar prospect. The sermon took 15 minutes to deliver, considerably longer than it would take for many of those listening to die after the whistles blew and the order to advance had been given.

On the eve of the Somme, the 29th of June 1916, the battalion was paraded and marched to their frontline positions through squads of Allied artillery units who cheered them on their way. The artillery barrage of the German lines had begun four days earlier, but so inaccurate was the bombardment that the PALS had to be guided carefully through it to minimise casualties resulting from so called *'friendly fire.'* The gunners weren't entirely to blame, of course: like the PALS they too in many cases were new and inexperienced. Nonetheless, many soldiers were killed or wounded by their own shells exploding within a few feet of them. Yet others were incapacitated by gas fired inexpertly from their own lines.

Yet to everyone in the war zone, a foot soldier heading for the front line should have been as recognisable as an army sergeant's stripes. On the back of Sonny's tunic was a star bearing the green and yellow colours of his battalion, and a patch of yellow cloth was also fixed to the flap of his haversack to enable the artillery to identify him in the heat of battle, and decide when the shell barrage should lift in line with how far forward the infantry had got. That at least was the theory, though experience in using 'lifting barrages' as a tactic was as limited as the expertise of the artillery units charged with instigating and managing them.

On top of his square of yellow cloth Sonny also had a brightly polished disc, the intention being to show aircraft overhead where he was on the battlefield. Pilots would then signal to the artillery who'd adjust their barrages as appropriate. Everything it seemed had been planned to synchronise with everything else, the product of the ordered military mind which, along with iron-discipline, had got Douglas Haig and his generals to where they were now. The only thing left was for officers to issue orders and soldiers to obey them. Trouble was, at the Battle of the Somme, one of war history's greatest acts of disorder, little of it worked as intended.

Encumbered with over 50 pounds of equipment added to by extra rounds of ammunition, Sonny and the 4th City PALS arrived in their support trenches 12 hours before zero with the deafening roar of artillery fire shaking the ground around them. The noise itself was terrifying and even a double ration of rum did little to mitigate it. At 5 a.m. on July 1st they rose from a sleepless night to a breakfast of dry bread, cheese and water. Between then and zero hour they put up trench bridges and ladders, took down their own barbed wire entanglements and were inspected, bizarrely you might think, as to their personal appearance. In the army's view soldiers smartly turned out was an indication of their high morale, a factor that counted for much in dispiriting the enemy. As a result, any soldier appearing in the trenches below the standards set by the army risked being charged with a punishable offence.

On being given the order to *'stand to'* and make ready for going over the top, most soldiers ordinarily did two things – lit a cigarette, then turned to shake hands with those alongside them. As he waited for the whistle to blow, one under-age recruit was often to be seen passing along as much trench as possible shaking hands with his comrades, weeping as he did so. There were other reactions that spoke just as clearly for men who understood only too well that in a few moments time they might be drawing their last breath. Some scribbled what could turn out to be their last letter home: others occupied themselves by putting on paper the hastily-assembled thoughts that in the event might be taken as being their last will and testament. Some stood in silent prayer or counted down the seconds: yet others simply wet themselves or shit their pants. If anyone entertained the notion, however fleeting, of refusing to go over the top or even dawdle in the process, they knew what the consequences would be. At the back of every unit in the frontline were military policemen with the powers to deal sternly with any laggards who looked like dragging their feet.

Like all major First World War battles, so much has been written about the Somme it would require a library of its own to accommodate it all. However, few speak more simply and directly about their experiences than those who took part in the encounter. Sometimes their accounts seem almost to understate the position they found themselves in considering the magnitude of the slaughter that was about to unfold: but they are never less than factual or guilty of hyperbole. Describing them as *'eloquent'* as some historians have done comes as close to patronising their authors as anything can. Only afterwards did poets talk of the *'fantastic shapes of struggling armies'*: for soldiers experiencing mass slaughter on the battlegrounds a different language (albeit with expletives deleted) was invoked as these two examples show.

'At 7.30 whistles were blown and the attack started. What did I see? To the left..and to the right..lines of soldiers going forward as though on parade in line formation. I reached the first German line and dropped into it where there were many German dead. The battlefield was nothing but shell-holes and barbed wire, but now I noticed many dead and dying and the lines of soldiers were not to be seen. With no officers or NCO near me I felt alone but still went forward from shell hole to shell hole. Later Corporal Beard joined me.

Things were now getting disorganised and at this point we could get no further. The machine gun fire was deadly. And our bombs had all been used up. The colonel of the Seaforths came up and took charge of all the odd groups of men belonging to various regiments. He told us to dig ourselves in and eventually there must have been 50 or 60 men at this spot, and it all started from the one small shell hole Corporal Beard and myself were first in.

At one time a shout went up that we were surrounded by Germans, but they were Germans running from dugouts in the first line and giving themselves up. I do not think they made it. With Corporal Beard we started to get back to our lines shell hole by shell hole, but we soon got parted. I managed to reach the British lines at 7.30 (p.m.), but the sight that met my eyes was terrible. Hundreds of dead soldiers everywhere...'

For those like Private Sidney Williamson who survived to write these passages, many did so at the cost of serious wounding, something that then became the concern of medical staff stationed at the rear. Here, the words of an un-named clergyman helping at a Casualty Clearing Station behind the lines, describes how the horror of the Somme started to unfold almost immediately the battle began:-

'7.30, the heavens and earth were rolling up, the crazy hour had begun...Aeroplanes dashed about, morning mist and gun smoke obscured the view. We got back from a late breakfast and soon the wounded by German shells came in, then all day long cars of dying and wounded... they are literally piled up, beds gone, lucky to get space on (the) floor of tent, hut or ward, and although the surgeons worked like Trojans many must yet die for lack of (an) operation. All the casualty clearing stations are overflowing.

Later.

We have 1,500 in and still they come..it is a sight..chaps with fearful wounds lying in agony, many so patient, some make a noise, one goes to a stretcher, lays one's hand on the forehead, it is cold, strike a match, he is dead – here a Communion, there an absolution, there a drink, there a madman, there a hot water bottle and so on – one madman was swearing and kicking, I gave him a drink, he tried to bite my hand and squirted water from his mouth into my face – well, it is an experience beside which all previous experience pales. Oh I am tired, excuse writing....'

That was committed to a diary kept by the padre through the first day of the Somme. By the third day, July 3rd, it was getting worse.

'Now I know something of the horrors of war. The (medical) staff is redoubled but what of that, imagine 1,000 badly wounded. The surgeons are beginning to get sleep, because after working night and day they realise we may be at this for some months...We hear of great successes but of course there are set backs and one hears of ramparts of dead English and Germans. Oh, if you could see our wards, tents, huts, crammed with terrible wounds – see rows of abdominals and lung penetrations...I get hold of some morphia and I go to that black hole of Calcutta, 'Moribund', and use it or creep into the long tents where two or three hundred Germans lie, you can imagine what attention they get with our own neglected, the cries and groans are too much to withstand and I cannot feel less pity for them than for our own. Surgeon and sisters are splendid and I go and bother them and they come without grumbling but one cannot drag them away from lifesaving to death-easing too often....'

For the Manchester PALS, the first day of the Somme was to provide equally unhinging experiences. Orders were for Sonny's battalion to lead the charge that would capture the crest of a low hill called the Glatz Redoubt. Once taken Glatz was to be held allowing the battalion to give covering fire to the other three Manchester PALS units who were to move through with their supporting detachments and take a further objective – the shell-wrecked town of Montabaun. The 4th City PALS succeeded in achieving everything asked of them, unarguably one of their most notable accomplishments in the entire war despite losing 190 of their number. From their elevated position at Glatz however, they were powerless to do other than watch as their comrades below fell like skittles in the face of entrenched German machine gun posts but they too got to their planned objective, arriving in Montabaun not far short of the appointed hour though probably bewildered as to why such a pile of shattered stones had ever become a desirable target in the first place.

In the days to follow Sonny was detailed to burying as many of his dead comrades as could be recovered from the stricken earth. Burial involved taking a dead soldier's equipment away and turning out his pockets. Then everything that might be returned to the regiment or his family was placed in the satchel that normally housed his gas helmet: his name and number was recorded by a supervising officer. Often a dead soldier had first to be dug from the shell hole he'd fallen into after being riddled by bullets or hit by shrapnel. Such was the devastation wrought that his identity tags were often the only reliable way of establishing who he was. Eventually, he'd be laid in a pit with anything up to 20 other bodies, his boots and uniform going with him. A few feet of earth covered the remains and a rough wooden cross was stuck at the head of the grave. Sonny stood bare-headed at the side of many a grave containing men he'd known well while the padre uttered the familiar words of committal - men like Cpl. George Holt for example, a lad around his own age who'd lived directly across the Stockport Road from where Sonny worked at Seymour Mead's. Another victim, a somewhat older PAL, Charlie Ollernshaw, worked for a local branch of Armstrong Whitworth in Manchester – a company whose business Charlie would know only too well was in the manufacture and sale of armaments.

On Tuesday the 4th of July Sonny's battalion was mustered for a roll call that revealed the true extent of their losses. At roll call the officer in charge called out a man's name to which the man responded if he was in a state fit enough to attend. If no response was forthcoming the officer would call his name a second time. If again there was no response the officer, features betraying nothing, eyes fixed firmly on the paper in his hand would take a note and pass on. By the end of the Somme's first week many boxes remained un-ticked: and in line with the empty spaces on the parade ground the note-taking grew.

Through to the second week of July Sonny was frequently in action, defending the gains made at Glatz and protecting his battalion from German counter-attacks on its flanks. After that, however, he was relieved and his battalion returned to billets and rest areas at the rear but by July 22nd the Manchester PALS were back on the frontline and the following day took part in an attack on the village of Guillemont. At dawn they went over the top and moved across open ground in wave-formation for a distance of around half-a-mile before capturing the village. The cost was losing all of their first and second waves – killed outright, wounded, or taken prisoner. Moving at walking pace and almost shoulder to shoulder into machine gun fire, the third and fourth waves of the 4th City PALS suffered badly before taking Guillemont although their commander, Henry Rawlinson, appeared to have no knowledge of their success. 'The Manchesters?' he asked with surprise. 'Are they in (Guillemont) now?' The officers around him nodded wearily. They were equally astonished he didn't already know.

Rawlinson, the general whose idea of the PALS in 1914 had given rise to new volunteer battalions across Britain, was to witness its total demise at the Somme less than two years later. Some like Sonny Boothroyd had survived, but so many others had perished that Rawlinson's grand scheme now lay buried with them in the chalky, uncompromising clay of Northern France. In mid-August he withdrew what was left of his volunteer soldiers from the immediate battle zone and dispatched them further north. Not one of the first four City PALS battalions raised at Manchester could muster even 500 men out of an original complement of over a 1000 soldiers. In the north, around the area of Bethune what was left of them went back into trenches – places whose mean, shallow indentations in waterlogged ground required massive sand-bagged protection front and back. Though they hardly qualified for the title of trenches, they were to be Sonny's first experience of coping with the life-sucking mud of Flanders.

As the Somme continued to take its toll, 25 miles away Douglas Haig went on exercising his horse – an equitation, which as an old cavalryman and polo player he did around the grounds of his chateau headquarters on every possible occasion. In the distance he could hear the rumble of artillery below the ceaseless piercing shrieks and detonating thuds of exploding shells: but only his mount, not Douglas, shied occasionally when the ground vibrated. *'Our troops are in wonderful spirits and full of confidence,'* he'd written on the eve of the Somme, mistaking the juvenile eagerness of the PALS for something more contiguous with the reality of the situation. Perhaps the *'spirits'* he referred to owed something to the distribution of the rum ration: at any rate, as battle commenced, *'confidence'* like the effects of the alcohol rapidly diminished. Haig's staff officers dutifully arrived in relays at his H.Q. passing on the assurances given to them by field commanders that everything was in the main going to plan. The battle, as Haig saw it, was now in the hands of his generals and there was little more he personally could do.

So adamant had Haig been that his overall plan for the Somme be adhered to, that he'd flatly rejected suggestions by some of his generals to experiment with what they considered as the perfectly valid approach of *'fire and movement'* in attack. This was where some soldiers lay down to cover others who then advanced through them – a type of leapfrogging technique that had shown its worth in other wars. Haig, as he frequently made clear, didn't want troops to lie down at any stage for the simple reason he thought they'd hesitate about getting up again. In one gruesome respect he was right. Thousands of soldiers, of course, did lie down at the Somme and didn't get up again: but that was because they were dead, in the words of one young officer, crawling into shell holes, wrapping themselves in a waterproof sheet and taking out their bibles before drawing their last breath. Haig's rigidity on other matters also prevailed at great cost in human lives. Advancing shoulder to shoulder in waves, each wave backing up the one in front by filling the gaps, was another order he gave that brooked no challenging. It mirrored the way the cavalry charged and Haig, being an old cavalryman himself, saw the process as being no different. *'The cavalry saved the British Empire,'* he is quoted as saying, with reference to his experiences in the Sudan War and elsewhere. Men and horses it seemed, were equally dispensable

In early October the Manchester PALS, their ranks only partly restored by new drafts of men, were moved back to the Somme to engage once again with the Germans near Bapaume. Despite the carnage the Somme campaign continued in the hopelessly optimistic belief that it would end with an Allied victory. On October 12th the 2nd City Pals went over the top in the battle of Transloy Ridges and were cut down before getting more than 20 yards from their starting position. 225 men and officers were accounted for by German machine gun fire. The 3rd City Pals who went over in support were similarly massacred losing 250 men. The next day the 1st City battalion was heavily shelled and gassed, leaving Sonny's unit to carry the wounded from the ridges to makeshift hospital facilities behind the lines. In the process of doing so they in turn were often overcome by gas shells exploding around them.

By mid-October Sonny's battalion was trying desperately to get supplies of ammunition and food to their comrades still occupying the forward trenches. As quickly as new trenches were dug many of them were blown in, often by shellfire from their own side falling short. Between them the artillery barrages coming from both sides in the battlefield only churned the wet clay even more, turning the entire area into a wasteland of flooded holes and treacherous mud.

On the 17th of October parts of Manchester's 1st City PALS moved up for a further attack largely ignorant of where the enemy's frontline was, and with little idea regarding the location of their machine-gun posts. Two hours before sunrise they went over the top, but by the time Sonny's battalion had arrived on the scene it was clear the attack had been a disaster. Moving in the dark had been like enduring a living nightmare. Men slid and stumbled in the quagmire, rifles and field guns jamming in the engulfing mud. Anyone falling into the string of water-filled shell holes barring the way was unlikely to be seen again. For four days Sonny spent most of his time thigh-deep in mud, exhausted and incapable of doing much more than wait for help to arrive. On the 21st the battalion was at last relieved and marched to the rear, but only after burying their comrades in the shallow ditches that passed for graves. Almost a hundred more Manchester PALS had been lost.

Philip Gibbs, one of five government approved journalists to witness events on the battlegrounds, was an observer at the Somme. Under the censoring eye of C.E. Montagu, Gibbs couldn't dispatch true eyewitness accounts of what he'd seen to his newspaper, the Daily Chronicle, but some time after the war ended he put his experiences on paper describing how he'd waded through the *'filth and stench of death'* to have a look at what soldiers like the Manchester PALS had unknowingly faced at the Somme immediately the order to attack had been given. He went down first into the deep fortifications the Germans had constructed on their side of the killing fields:

'Our men did not build like this. This German industry was a rebuke to us – yet we had captured their work, and the dead bodies of their labourers lay in those dark caverns, killed by our bombers...I drew back from those fat corpses. They looked monstrous, lying there crumpled up amongst a foul litter of clothes, stick bombs, old boots and bottles'.

Moving back to the surface, the dual emotions of awe and shock continued to assail him:

'Groups of dead lay in ditches which had once been trenches...they had been bayoneted. I remember one man – an elderly fellow - sitting up with his back to a bit of earth with his hands half raised. He was smiling a little, though he had been stabbed through the belly and was stone dead.

Victory!...Some of the German dead were young boys, too young to be killed for old men's crimes, and others might have been old or young. One could not tell because they had no faces, and were just masses of raw flesh in rags of uniforms. Legs and arms lay separate without any bodies thereabouts'.

The Somme campaign ended in November 1916 almost where it had begun. Most of the new Allied front line lay barely three miles from the old, and along half the original front no significant movement had occurred at all. In the process the Allies had lost 600,000 men... the Germans around the same number. However, with DORA breathing down their necks the newspapers at home were persuaded to present the Somme as a victory of sorts, although no one dared go as far as calling for celebrations in the streets. Only Haig, his generals and their counterparts in the German military knew the real extent of the savagery, and they were keeping schtumm. The politicians, so they claimed, only learned of the horrors some time after the war had moved on to even greater calamities. As for the troops, who, like Sonny Boothroyd had survived the bloodbath, there was hardly time to reflect and gather their energy before preparations for a new Allied offensive were being thrust upon them. Not too far along the line, though plenty more killing was to come in the meantime, the Battle of Passchendaele awaited.

Chapter 14

'Brilliant to the top of his army boots,' was how Lloyd George came to describe Douglas Haig, Commander-in-Chief of British forces on the Western Front and the man who ordered the Battle of the Somme. And in case we hadn't already got the point, the wartime Prime Minister added, *'he was a man devoid of the gift of intelligent and coherent expression.'* Winston Churchill, who knew Haig better than most was only marginally less disparaging in his assessment of the field marshall. *'He surely was'* Churchill declared, *'unequal to the prodigious scale of events.'* Other people, however, less-elevated and inclined towards calling a spade a spade, were more direct in their use of language. Haig, they said, was the *'Butcher of the Somme.'*....

In keeping with this allusion to butchery and the slaughterhouse, First World War historians have continued to carve up Haig's reputation over the years producing a variorum of views that portray him as a blunderer, a dinosaur, a man with the obstinacy of an ox, and someone whose mind was as open to innovation and new ideas on warfare as a heavily-fortified German pillbox. He has his supporters too of course: and apologists but Haig has drawn more criticism than praise in the decades following the end of the war, and the line taken on his personality defects still tend to dominate, put forward as the reasons for him coldly committing so many young men to death and destruction on the battlefields of Europe. Yet elements of doubt continue to hover above most of the conclusions drawn from all the dissections made of Haig's character. Is it possible for one man to be all the things historians claim he was? We emerge only a little wiser from our history books, feeling encouraged to despise him without being sure we fully understand why. Historians have re-routed the Haig narrative so often we wonder if it's ever going to be possible to reach a satisfactory conclusion about him.

Any rational assessment of Haig's actions in the First World War has to start with his formative experiences as an army officer on the battlegrounds, especially his involvement in the Sudan wars and those in South Africa. Douglas Haig was invited by Kitchener (not ordered, you'll note) to join Britain's campaign in the late 1890s against the Sudanese separatists, the legendary Dervishes, who had mobilised against British and French land-grabbing in neighbouring Egypt where many of their fellow countrymen lived. Haig, as a cavalry officer, commanded troops at two major battles in the Sudan, those at Atbara and Omdurman. The Battle of Omdurman signalled the final rout of the Sudanese tribesmen, bringing the war to an end, whereupon Kitchener occupied the city of Khartoum and established control over a country almost the size of Europe.

However, the price paid by the defeated separatist army was not to be met merely in terms of the thousands of them who were slain. Those who'd survived being killed outright were then callously bayoneted and shot where they lay on the ground, something that moved Churchill, also a serving officer in Sudan, to write in a letter to his wife *'...the victory at Omdurman was disgraced by the inhuman slaughter of the wounded and that Kitchener was responsible for this.'*

Untroubled by such criticism Kitchener then proceeded to order the tomb of the venerated Islamic leader, Al-Mahadi, to be destroyed and his remains burned before having his ashes thrown in the Nile. Everything but his skull was to be disposed of in this way, because Kitchener had other plans for it: he wanted to mount it in silver and use it as a drinking cup. Only the intervention of other, less-unbalanced people around Kitchener persuaded him to retract this order and to have the skull buried in a nearby Moslem cemetery.

All of these excesses on and around the Sudanese battlefields were witnessed by Douglas Haig. Also in attendance as it happened were Henry Rawlinson and Marshall Joseph Joffre - both destined to play major roles in the First World War. Rawlinson commanded the PALS at the Somme and Joffre was Haig's equivalent for a time in the French army. On the eve of the First World War Joffre declared, *'As in the Sudan, I have always succeeded in whatever I do. It will be that way again.'* And like Haig, Joffre was recognised as someone incapable of admitting defeat and for brushing away the cost in casualties resulting from the inconclusive battles he ordered to be fought. In a message to French troops on the Western Front he urged them to recognise that, *'The hour has come to advance at all costs and to die where you stand rather than give way.'* Such was the temperament of the generals surrounding Haig in the Sudan.

Barely a year after the Sudan however, Kitchener was taking his leave of North Africa and with Haig at his side travelling south towards another cause of concern for Britain's land-grabbers – The Transvaal and Orange Free State. British colonialists in South Africa, like Cecil Rhodes, anticipated their arrival with no little delight. Having tried and failed to invade the two states that contained the biggest goldfields in the world, Rhodes and those around him had stood down their personal armies of paramilitaries, and now looked to their old country's regular army under Kitchener to do the job for him. What became known as the Boer Wars were about to begin.

On the long journey south Douglas Haig, eleven years younger than his mentor was ever keen to listen to what the doyen of the military had to say. Though he would in time turn on Kitchener asserting that only the ineptness of the Sudanese had lost them the war. At the time there was still much Haig could learn from a man whose unsparing brutality in the Sudan had not stood in the way of him being elevated to the peerage: Kitchener was now Lord Kitchener of Khartoum.

Tucked away in Haig's mind as he buffed his boots and talked about horses, were things that he'd observed in battle that would shortly be added to in even more horrendous detail. The famously dull and uncommunicative Haig must have reflected much on what he'd experienced under Kitchener's command in the Sudan, and how in war politicians and public opinion were wont to forgive excesses providing the result went their way in the end. To his peers Haig continued being the quiet one of the group around Kitchener, shy even in some people's estimation. After an interview with a journalist from the Daily Mail, he was described as being as *'shy as a schoolgirl.'* Fortunately, Winston Churchill wasn't asked at the time for his opinion on this estimate of Haig's character. *'Some shyness!'* he might have said. *'Some schoolgirl!'*

Prior to the Boer War land-grabbers of several European countries had been busy in South Africa for many years. Colonialists from Britain, Holland and France had already divided the area into separate fiefdoms, Britain grabbing the lands of Natal and Cape Colony, the Dutch a mix of other territories including Transvaal. In the process the previous owners of these territories – the indigenous black Africans – had been given short shrift, left to scratch a living from ground worthless and unwanted by the colonisers, or else employed in back-breaking labour for their masters at bare subsistence wages. If they failed to comply with either option they were bullied at gunpoint, or simply left to decay…a choice of rot or shot. The human energy needed for exploiting the riches of South Africa allowed little time or latitude to those who might have different ideas about how their country should be developed and, of course, Cecil Rhodes was all for replacing them with *'human capital'* – the surplus population of Britain who were threatening bloody civil war at home.

When the biggest goldfield on the globe was discovered near Pretoria in 1887, however, the existing relationships between neighbouring land-grabbers changed, and they decided to put aside their belief in sharing the country's riches and embark on a quite different steer altogether. To the obvious delight of Cecil Rhodes, thousands of British people uprooted themselves and settled in South Africa – part of a goldrush that had the prospect of freeing them from the constant round of poverty and deprivation at home. Although they didn't know it, the land-grabbers had other plans for them beyond that.

The gold lay within the territory of the Boers, descendants of the original Dutch settlers, and if historians are to be believed, the influx of British found themselves paying taxes to the Boer government but with no rights in deciding how they were spent. It was the age-old case of taxation without representation being used to stir up discontent. The 'injustice' of collecting taxes from un-enfranchised citizens, however, was no more than a flimsy excuse for one lot of colonialists (the British) to lay hold of territory belonging to another lot of colonialists (the Boers), and in doing so get their hands on the gold. In 1895 Cecil Rhodes had financed a raid from a strip of land lying alongside the Transvaal, hoping it would provide the opening for the private soldiers of his British South Africa Company to occupy the Boer state. The raid, known as the Jameson Raid after the Scot who led it, failed, hence the expectation that Kitchener would do better. Surrounded by the myths of 'justice' and 'fairness' for the British in Transvaal, therefore, the Boer War began.

The most horrifyingly brutal phase of the Boer War came at the end of the year 1900. The Boers had adopted guerrilla techniques, something the British hadn't met with before and it unsettled them. The guerrillas under arms left their homes and took to the countryside, attacking the British in surprise raids then melting away in the night. Kitchener was at a loss. Having anticipated a short war fought along traditional lines, he now faced an insurgency that looked like having no foreseeable end. Drastic action was required and Kitchener didn't hesitate before instigating it.

First he stripped the land of anything that might conceivably help the Boers. It was a scorched earth policy of killing livestock, burning farms, destroying crops and poisoning the water supply. Almost 40 settlements were razed to the ground along with 30,000 farms. Known as someone who *'would sacrifice everything to the business in hand'*, his orders to blow up buildings at times resulted in the deaths of his own men. In being told on one occasion that five of his men had been killed in one such action, he cabled back to the officer in charge, *'Do you want any more dynamite?'*

When his scorched earth policy failed to deter the guerrillas, Kitchener finally turned to attempted genocide. As he saw it by wiping out the wherewithal of creating future generations, the enemy would never have the means of returning to challenge him. It was attempted mass murder on Kitchener's part, the process of eliminating an entire national group. Central to that process were his generals, amongst them Douglas Haig.

They were ordered to round up non-combatants, mainly women and children and place them in *'concentration camps.'* Truthfully, there was little to distinguish them from death camps although death for those incarcerated was to come slowly over many months. Photographs existing today show the plight of Boer women and children, dying in stages from undernourishment and starvation in rough shelters that gave no protection against the winter cold. Half-rations killed the children, the heartbreak of losing them contributing hugely to the death of their mothers. It is estimated that around one-quarter of the Boer population was murdered in this way along with 120, 000 black Africans.

The journalist William Stead, one of the closed circle surrounding Cecil Rhodes, was to comment that the camps, *'..were nothing more than a cruel torture machine,'* and their use in the Boer War gave rise to international outrage and condemnation. Cemeteries containing the victims of a land-grabbing feud that reached sinister new levels of brutality, are today the scene for commemoration services in South Africa although they fail to impress everyone. A few years ago, Dr. Saul Bellow, an expert in modern South African history, said in a BBC interview that although, *'overall the British were the aggressors (in the Boer War), the primary blame for deaths in the concentration camps has much more to do with incompetence and lack of medical care than a deliberate attempt to kill'*. He added that demands for an apology from Britain were *'specious'* and reduced history to a morality tale that served no useful purpose.

His words have the historian's familiar Haig-like ring to them – incompetence, blundering, not things to be confused with a planned campaign to murder. Haig, of course, present at all that went on in South Africa would say nothing until he came to write his memoirs. That was his style. He was a hardened soldier after all, further inured by the Boer War to suffering and death even when it was inflicted on civilians and people too young to have had any part in the causes of it.

However, his experiences in the Sudan and South Africa would have provided him with lots to reflect on: an amorphous image that in days to come would look decidedly normal from his angle of view. In some ways he had Kitchener to thank for that, someone who'd taught him that flexibility in the military species could at times be useful, even if it meant less than perfect adaptation to the permanent realities of war. Kitchener, the great 'cut and dried' specialist would continue to lead the army, as would Douglas Haig in the fullness of time, doing what they both knew to be right. There would be other wars, other conflicts where people were put to the sword. Haig, like the good cavalryman he was always kept his own sword immaculately clean and polished. You never could tell when you'd be called upon to use it.

Chapter 15

Dead soldiers when Sonny was a kid didn't stay 'dead' for long. The hard, frequently aqueous pavements of Manchester were no place for a child to feign death for any longer than a few minutes at a time. Miraculously, the stricken 'soldier' would groan and rise to his feet clutching an arm or a leg. When he'd persuaded the rest of the gang to accept that he'd only been 'wounded' the game would resume with all its previous enthusiasm.

The Boothroyd kids, like children living in all Britain's industrial towns and cities, viewed the streets and alleys around their neighbourhood as one vast playground. Overcrowding and the effects of confined spaces on sibling rivalries meant the streets offered an opportunity for escape - not least from the stern and unrelenting eye of a disciplinarian father. The streets by contrast held the promise of challenge and adventure not to say the scope for being naughty without inviting more than the token wrath of a passing grown-up. And playing in the dirt might also have had advantages educationally in terms of preparation for entering primary school. There you began learning the skills of writing by scratching with a stick in a trough of clayey-sand before being allowed access to a slate or the expensive paper hoarded by the teacher.

Skipping with ropes, throwing quoits and whipping spinning tops till they sang were just some of the games popular with children at the time the Boothroyds were kids. They went along with swapping cigarette cards and comics: and if you were in any sort of favour with an older brother he might just lend a hand in building you a cart made from a wooden crate fixed to some old pram wheels. Needless to say, however, the same pattern of gender-driven behaviour prevailed in Sonny's childhood days as it continued to do for several generations to come. Boys climbed lamp-posts and jumped from high walls: girls on the other hand did daft things like dressing dolls and developing their minds by talking to them.

Street lighting fuelled by gas came to Manchester at the end of the 19th century, providing children with another avenue of play that hadn't existed previously. To light the gas lamps required a man to go around with a long pole charged at its tip with an ignition substance, calcium carbide. The lamplighter pushed the pole through a gap in the underside of the lamp and the calcium carbide proceeded to light the gas mantle. Children were fascinated by the whole process and followed the lamplighter around waiting for the darkness to be vanquished by the soft, gleaming light. They were also keen on obtaining the spent carbide that the lamplighter dumped in the gutter when most of the life had gone out of it. It still contained enough fizz, however, to entertain the kids who poured water on it causing it to bubble and froth. Children were beguiled by the display until the awful stench of the carbide drove them away.

Another popular distraction, though only marginally less noisy and energetic than other street games, was to kneel in front of a sweet shop window and say what you would buy if you had the wealth to do so. A list of ten favourites was allowed...five if you were playing with anyone less than your best pals. Lists were reeled out subject to endless revisions based on the shape and colour of the confectionery displayed. Expensive Belgian chocolate and Turkish Delight would figure prominently at the outset: but gradually children reverted to the things they'd already tasted and enjoyed most, usually four-for-a-farthing caramels, liquorice laces, and halfpenny sherbet dabs. Choices would be enunciated at high volume and great speed until with no one listening very much to what anyone else was saying, the game would be wound up. For the Boothroyds games such as this would have carry-over effects on later life. Sonny's older brother Frank would eventually become the proprietor of his own sweet shop in Stanley Grove. It may even have been one in front of which he had knelt as a child.

Loitering outside the pub door waiting for the boozers to emerge was another childhood activity to be observed in working class Manchester and other industrial centres. A spare copper left over from the night's drinking sometimes stood a chance of rolling in the direction of a waiting child. The same went for children who chose to hang about places of entertainment when audiences debouched on to the pavements. Trouble was you had to scramble for the money in competition with your peers, not to say the occasional adult 'pauper' also waiting for a charitable feeling or two to manifest themselves. In Sonny's day a pauper was someone on poor relief, unemployed and a client of the Poor Law. Even at home they were unable to conceal their penurious state from others. The sparse furnishings...the worn lino...the small iron grate with its plain wooden shelf above...were, of course, invisible to all but the occupants but the windows were often the giveaway. If paper rather than curtains was used to keep prying eyes at bay, that was enough to tell the world of your social standing. Paper, the grey flag of poverty, said it all.

As the Boothroyd kids grew towards their teens the invitation to involve themselves in more structured activities presented itself. Joining the Scouts or the Boys Brigade was an option many took: but most dropped out soon after taking their oath to God and King and learning how to salute their officers. Many children found membership of these quasi-military organisations disappointing because of all the tedious marching and drilling that followed induction, especially in the Boys Brigade. What took place at the drill hall on mid-week evenings seemed remote from what had been promised in the way of outdoor adventures: and the occasional camping trip, overseen by the censorious eye of an adult patrol leader, was no compensation for the lost freedom of the streets.

The performances staged at Manchester's Belle Vue Gardens on the other hand influenced much of what children did in their street games. Belle Vue was just a short walk from the Boothroyd's house in Stanley Grove and offered a wide range of distractions including a zoo, tea pavilions, pleasure-grounds and in summer, outdoor ballroom dancing. It was massively popular amongst all the city's social classes, and its theatrical performances normally attracted full houses. Many of Belle Vue's stage productions, however, were Empire-orientated and presented in a matrix of muscular Christianity, flag waving and militarism. Even so, at the time Sonny Boothroyd was leaving school and joining Seymour Mead, the straight-jacket of this social Puritanism was beginning to fray at the seams.

Kids' games were moving on, and increasingly away, from what their parent's generation viewed as wholesome and edifying entertainment. Games now were reflecting a wider range of activities drawn in many cases from the everyday experiences surrounding children. Steam trains had always fascinated children and their hissing, puffing and fiery ways had always had a presence in street games. Now this was being added to by the advent of motorised transport - cars and buses, the latter having been introduced to Manchester in 1906 when Sonny was twelve and, of course, fanaticism for football was growing all the time.

Both the big Manchester football clubs, United and City, were making good progress up through the League tables. By the time of the First World War, Manchester City were prospering more than their rivals finishing 3rd in the upper division as against United who were 3rd from the bottom. Professional football, however, was only like the sugar-coating on the sweet shop's confectionery. Boys were taking to the streets more and more with a ball at their feet. The ball was rarely the size of a regulation football, and didn't always have a lace that foreshadowed facial disfigurement: but it was enough to provide for games in the streets frequently played by enough boys to populate a small village. As legend would have us believe, out of this came the great players of the future whose skills were to grace the likes of Wembley stadium.

On Good Friday 1915, however, professional football came to a halt and remained in limbo for the duration of the First World War. Manchester United's last meaningless match against Liverpool ended in scandal, several players on both sides being subsequently charged with match-fixing. Not that the kids playing in the cities streets seemed bothered by malpractice. Falsely claiming to have been fouled when really you'd just missed a sitter in front of goal was not an uncommon occurrence. You lay there groaning and holding your head. But as the game raged on around you, a small miracle arrived to enable you to recover and resume playing. The streets of Manchester were as cold and hard for the footballer as they had been for the stricken soldier of the previous day.

Chapter 16

'So how long have you been in then?'

The soldier alongside Sonny juggles with his rifle and blows into each of his cupped hands trying to restore some circulation to his numbed fingers. The 19th battalion are on the move again despite word that the issues causing the previous delay have not been fully resolved.

'Over two years since I got me call-up papers,' Sonny replies. *'That meant I got me proficiency pay last April.'*

His companion looks up at the dark Flanders sky, heavy now with the threat of snow. *'Well, there aint much to spend it on around 'ere. You can't even get a bloody rag for cleanin' your rifle. The other day I 'ad to make do by cutting a strip off the tail o' me shirt.'* His eyes gleam angrily in the inky darkness. *'It's a shocker what we 'ave to put up with out 'ere.'*

Every day, whether it needs it or not, an infantryman's rifle has to be taken apart, cleaned and oiled. It's seen as a means to maintaining discipline and order, and like many other army routines is often a complete waste of time. Getting your hair cut and being clean-shaven are other rules enforced with little leniency. Soldiers failing to conform risk a field punishment which can mean being tied to the wheel of a gun limber for several hours at a time. Persistent offenders can expect several hours of this treatment over several days. In March, 1917, only too aware of the consequences of appearing on parade unshaven, Sonny wrote to his mother:

'There is one thing I should like and that's a safety razor and one or two blades. Frank will know what sort I mean. They was not very dear, or rather they was not dear while I was in blighty. Of course things have altered now, everything has gone dearer.'

A few weeks later he got what he needed inside a parcel from the ever-obliging Sarah, although she'd asked one of her son's younger friends to choose the razor for her. *'It's a very good one,'* Sonny wrote back. *'Thank Alf very much from me as I don't know his address.'* Alf, whose poor physical health had saved him from conscription, would probably never know just how much potential aggravation he'd spared his chum.

'If you've been in that long,' the soldier continues *'how come you're still in one piece? There's many hasn't got as far as you 'ave without running into some sort of trouble.'*

Sonny points to his shoulder. *'I've 'ad me share. Caught a bit of shrapnel 'ere a few weeks ago, and this time last year I was in hospital with trench foot.'* The soldier frowns. *'They says it's no joke that trench foot. They says if you don't catch it in time a bloke can lose his whole foot in the end.'* He drums his own feet quietly on the duckboards. *'Mind you, I wouldn't mind a spell in 'ospital if it meant getting shot of this fuckin' place for a while.'*

Trench foot is an infection that had put upwards of 20,000 soldiers on the casualty list during the first five months of the war. It remained a threat for all servicemen who spent long hours standing in mud and water without the facilities afterwards to dry out properly. Unbelievably, in the early days the military viewed it as a symptom of 'poor morale' and stayed sceptical even when trench foot was diagnosed as a fungal infection derived from conditions on the battlefield and capable of causing serious nerve and muscle damage. A soldier's feet became swollen and cold to touch: and pain, itching and a feeling like chronic pins and needles would follow. Left untreated it could lead to gangrene and amputation. To be hospitalised for any significant period usually meant the condition had reached serious levels, and Sonny Boothroyd realised in advance he was in trouble when he wrote in November 1916:

'Dear mother...just a line in answer to your letter which I received while in the trenches. I could not very well write because I have not been so well lately myself this last week or two. The trenches are in a bad condition at present, in some parts they are above the knees in water and mud and we have a job to walk through it. So you may tell when we come out we are about jiggered up fit for nothing and I'm sorry to keep you such a while without writing...'

A month later he was adding a postscript, this time from a hospital bed behind the lines. *'Just to let you know*

I am not keeping so bad although I'm in hospital. Have got a dose of trench foot...'

Before being dispatched to hospital Sonny had a field ticket attached to him giving his name and number. In the overflowing wards of the makeshift hospitals at the rear, this means of identification was necessary in a situation where wounded men were often laid side by side on the floor awaiting assessment and decisions about their treatment. Every bed, every palette, every trestle and bare timber board was utilised to accommodate the sick and injured, and thereafter each patient was addressed by his number rather than by name.

Men caked in filth from the battlegrounds were initially examined by male doctors then treated by women – nurses assisted by volunteer auxiliaries known as VADs. VADs did the donkey-work, nurses the treatment of wounds and illnesses. In an inversion of the rigid social structures at home, the usually middle-class VADs carried out the lowly routine chores, freeing the mainly working class nurses for duties requiring higher levels of skill. But there was no distinction made when it was time for them to find somewhere to rest after a long shift. Often they slept in holes dug under the floors of their living quarters, a sheet of corrugated iron their only protection from shrapnel and other debris resulting from the enemy's wayward shell bombardments.

Working class men of the First World War era were unused to hospitals since only charities offered help to those unable to pay: so they were uncomfortable in the presence of so many uniformed females. Shyness manifested itself in different forms, most often in unwonted rudeness or constant complaints about the routines hospital demanded of them. But feelings of vulnerability lay at the heart of their reactions to their female carers, increasing the determination to appear as a soldier should in any situation. Those who could struggle into a sitting position despite the pain did so: and it was almost a matter of personal dignity and pride to shave your own cheeks and even if confined to bed, wear a collar and tie.

Many battlefield casualties didn't make it beyond hospital, dying as a result of the emergency operations they underwent or from infections arising from them. Morphine as a painkiller was in such short supply that only those in extreme distress were administered it. For amputated stumps that turned septic a solution of eusol and peroxide was poured on in an attempt to let the pus out. It rarely worked and often it seemed less hellish to suffer than to go on enduring the agony of the treatment prescribed.

Sometimes the nurses themselves were traumatised by the cases with which they had to deal. Many gassed soldiers, for example, were already beyond hope when they arrived in the wards, lungs and eyes often horribly damaged from being in the vicinity of exploding gas shells. In chlorine gas attacks, hydrochloric acid was formed immediately it came into contact with the moisture contained in the human body. Lungs, like flesh, could be damaged beyond repair. One nurse attending a soldier through his last hours remembered:

'He was sitting up in bed fighting for breath, his lips plum-coloured. I shall never forget the look on his face as he turned to me and gasped 'I can't die! Is it possible nothing can be done for me?' It was a horrible death, but as hard as they tried doctors were unable to find a way of successfully treating chlorine gas poisoning..'

Total gas casualties in the First World War have been estimated at around 1.25 million, although in recent times attempts have been made to minimize the effects of chemical weapons used in the First World War by pointing out that only 3 per cent of victims actually died from gas, ignoring the rest who suffered debilitating conditions for the rest of their lives rendering them unfit for any sort of work or engaging with normal human activities.

No medical record remains of Sonny Boothroyd's stay in hospital: but he spent the best part of three months being treated for trench foot which suggests serious problems, and he may well have suffered the amputation of some toes. In times past this would have meant a 'blighty' – a return to England for more treatment and convalescence with his family in Manchester. By 1917 however, home leave was being greatly restricted because of the need to return men quickly to their fighting units. There was also concern over troops returning from leave bringing with them de-vitalising reports about life on the home front. Food shortages, industrial unrest, questions about the conduct of the war and how it was being reported, were all things the military top brass were keen to keep out of the trenches. Breaking into soldier's mail now became a matter beyond mere censorship, and evolved rapidly into a means of measuring the morale of those preparing for further battles on the Western Front. In many ways it could be seen as a vast survey of how the troops now felt about the war.

On March 2nd 1917, Sonny was sent back to his battalion - *'feeling a lot better now'* as he wrote to his mother shortly afterwards. Apart from a field postcard, he'd not been in contact with Stanley Grove for the best part of three months. In his first proper letter home he told Sarah Boothroyd *'I have been back with the regiment for over a week now and I find it very hard coming out of hospital straight back to the battalion.'* If he expected time to adjust again to life in the trenches, he was surely to be disappointed. Sonny and his re-engagement with both the Germans and the Flanders weather was to start very shortly after his return to active service. On April 9th the planned battles around the town of Arras would explode into life...

'Well, at least it's quieter tonight,' the soldier beside him now says, *'though you never know what the Bosche 'as in mind. Even when their doing nothing, you reckon they must be up to fuckin summat.'*

Sonny glances down at the man's feet. His boots and puttees look in good condition compared with his own worn and grubby accoutrements. He guesses they might well have been taken from a dead soldier. Whereas arms, ammunition, any tools and equipment belonging to a fallen soldier had by order to be collected and returned to the rear, clothing and footwear were a different matter. Even if it was the custom to bury a man in his boots and uniform if something looked like fitting you, you took it especially if it was obviously superior to what you possessed at the time. A dead man's boots...part of a fallen soldier's uniform...there were no great feelings of abhorrence any more. And why should there be? The best designed uniform on earth, it was said, was no protection against the long slow chill of death.

The soldier next to Sonny yawns and stretches, beating his arms across his chest to inspire some warmth. *'Christmas, eh?'* he says. *'Who would believe it! This time at 'ome I'd be tuckin' into yesterday's leftovers. Now what 'ave I got to look forward to? Bully beef stew and mouldy biscuits!'* Pausing to light a fresh cigarette from the stub still burning between his fingers, he glances back along the trench before returning bitterly to his favourite theme. *'Will them that 'as the power never put and end to this bloody war?'*

Sonny shrugs and pulls his collar higher around his neck. *'Any signs of it being over in blighty?'* he'd asked in a letter home exactly one month previously. From what he gathers from his mother's reply there's little hope. *'When it does come to a finish though,'* he tells the soldier, *'you can bet we'll be the last to know.'* He thinks briefly of his upcoming birthday, prays that it might be his last in khaki. In 1896, the year he was born, the shortest war in world history took place, ironically one between Britain and Germany over who should possess the African colony of Zanzibar. It took all of 38 minutes for the victorious British to decide the matter - less time than it took for the likes of Sonny and most of his comrades to be enlisted in the army of the First World War.

Chapter 17

Had Sonny been granted a recuperative-spell of home leave in Manchester, he would certainly have visited his old place of work on the corner of the Stockport Road. There, within Seymour Mead's, he would have found things greatly changed. The combined effects of volunteering and conscription had taken its toll on the younger members of staff, leaving just a few older men behind the counter helped out by errand boys and part-time female employees. It was as if this decline in their ranks was keeping pace with the decline of stock items appearing on the grocer's shelves. A German U-boat blockade of the Channel Ports was having its desired effects, and essential food supplies were either slow in getting through to Britain's towns and cities, or else lay at the bottom of the sea.

Staple foodstuffs such as meat, butter and sugar were soon to be delivered to multiple stores like Mead's in strict rotation, though shoppers didn't always know in advance which one was next in line for its quota. When any definite news emerged it travelled at the speed of a torpedo, and the shop concerned soon came under siege often by children sent by mothers who hoped their youthful entreaties would soften the shopkeeper's heart enough to allow a little extra to find its way into the grocery bag. The ruse rarely worked, however. Shops became powerless to dispense more than the amounts given to them, or make anything in the way of concessions to those in dire need. Anyway, where a child did succeed in coaxing an extra spoonful of something out of the grocer, there was no guarantee it would survive the journey home, especially if the 'something' happened to be sweet, like sugar.

The quota system meant that Seymour Mead would be sent say a cask of butter or round of cheese to sell, whereupon the shop would close while staff reduced the bulk material to more-conveniently sized packages. After building them into stacks on the counter the doors were reopened and the onslaught began. The British habit of queuing didn't start with the First World War, but the war surely provided it with its severest test to date. It was almost beyond human endurance to wait patiently in a line stretching down the street, only to find when you got to the counter most of what your family needed had gone. Soon however, this sort of experience would become a thing of the past when food rationing complete with ration books was piloted by several local authorities in England. By April 1918 it had been extended to the entire nation.

Long before the First World War, competition between Seymour Mead and the other multiples had been nothing short of cut-throat. Stores like Lipton's, Home & Colonial and Maypole led the pack, but lesser-lights like Meadow Dairies and Mead's forever sought ways of leaching customers away from the big guns by posing as providers to a broad social spectrum within their localities. Operating on the same commercial basis as each other – buying in bulk and selling cheap – the multiples shared only one other thing in common...a hatred for the Co-op with its 'socialistic' shareholdings and annual dividends which went into the purses of its members instead of the proprietors pockets. They shouldn't have worried. The turnover from volume selling provided tidy profits for the multiples, and in time they grew into stores offering a greater variety of goods than the Co-op.

Up to 1914 you could buy almost every foodstuff you needed from a local branch of the multiples, from flea powder to fine wines, from lentils and liquorice to luxury boiled ham. It was said of John Sainsbury, whose multiple stores eventually grew into an empire of supermarkets, that he raised the humble cheesemongers shop to the dignity of a profession. It was a model that smaller retailers like Seymour Mead strove to emulate, not least in the area of human resource development which began when a new employee joined the firm.

In serving his apprenticeship as a grocer Sonny was expected to acquire a broad range of skills that included giving customers advice on preparing and cooking food and what to look for when choosing wines and spirits. He would also be coached in the ways of encouraging better-off customers towards more high-end lines of merchandise. He was expected always to remain courteous, honest and personally accountable for all he did. One of the few responsibilities he wouldn't be given, however, was arranging customer credit. That remained a task for senior management or the proprietors themselves, though credit was to become a thorn in the side of all retailers whose richer customers, unlike ordinary people, hardly ever paid in cash. At one point in the late-1880s such was the level of debt being incurred by the better off, that stores like Harrods ceased offering credit facilities altogether.

All of this was a long way from what the small corner shops and street markets of the time were able to provide, although both continued being a source of supply for the many working class families who went in search of their daily sustenance. In amongst the market stalls which offered live poultry, freshly killed rabbits, animal tripe and potato pie, you'd have been surprised to find a grocer's apprentice like Sonny Boothroyd putting himself at your service. More likely it would be the shrill calls of the bread and bun makers that assailed your ears along with the humbug sellers, quack medicine men and those offering a cure for just about every human ailment all mixed up in the general melee of kids, caged birds and captive household pets. At the multiples like Seymour Mead, fresh salmon and French brie might be a choice if your bank account measured-up to the size of your epicurean palate. In the street market pork ribs and cabbage was about as grand as it got, sold to you in an enamel basin for fourpence.

Yet Seymour Mead was not unaware of the benefits that accrued from trading in foodstuffs that seemed more suited to the outdoor markets, and had no difficulty in adding them to their stock. They also took care in choosing where to locate their stores, positioning them as close to the crossroads of the social divide as possible. While rival multiples seized on sites in and around the city centre, Mead went for those that sat astride the boundary line separating industrial communities from suburbia. That way they could trade with both sections of the population – working class and toffs. The lower end of Manchester's Longsight district where the Boothroyds lived provided an ideal location in that respect.

Longsight was no less a creature of Manchester's involvement with the Industrial Revolution than any other part of the city. It had little in the way of navigable rivers or canals, so mills and factories were not a feature of its landscape. Its existence was due to railways, and if it was renowned for anything it was surely the huge locomotive sheds and marshalling yards located in the northern part of its parish. The result was that pollution which blew across other parts of South Manchester was absent for much of the time, and soon streets of desirable homes within easy reach of the rail system began appearing - Manchester's own version of Metroland where many of the wealthier middle-class decided to live.

These southern suburbs sat little more than a mile from the bottom end of the Stockport Road: and it was at the bottom end of the Stockport Road that Seymour Mead chose to put their store. Other advantages of locating there was the less-onerous burdens of rent and rates levied on premises closer to the city centre, and it avoided direct competition with the bigger retailers who operated there. It also enabled a business to become more acquainted with those who populated suburbia, those living in grander properties and enjoying a grander lifestyle by dint of higher salaries derived from grander occupations. They, in many cases were the prototype parents of the PALS, people with contacts that could lead to those with power in the city, people who might do you favours, who effected introductions, who could be useful in easing the way to greater commercial success if that was what you aimed for. The pre-war period was one that saw Seymour Mead steadily growing their chain of grocery stores, a chain that now spread outward from Manchester to towns like Lytham and Stockport, and ultimately to the coastal town of Waterloo in the far flung reaches of Lancashire. Like the coffee-shop chains of modern times, once a beach-head had been established in any of these locations more outlets were sure to follow.

As employers though, Seymour Mead might have hoped for more reward than they actually got from encouraging employees like Sonny Boothroyd to enlist for service in the First World War. Like other Manchester-based businesses they held workplace gatherings where the virtues of courage in volunteering for the war were extolled. However, unlike textile magnates such as Tootal's and cartels like the Fine Cotton Spinners who seemed to have free license to continue using-up vital supplies of coal and shipping and retaining staff as yet un-conscripted by the munitions industry, Mead's ended up with food rationing and frequently empty shelves. The belief that leading the recruitment drive would mean grist-to-the-mill and pounds-in-the-till was turning out to be a dud one, which no amount of networking with influential contacts could overcome.

In the trenches their employees were eking-out a frugal existence with food none of which would have made it over the threshold of Seymour Mead's premises. Bread made from ground-up turnip: soups and stews suspected of containing horse meat: and indigestible corned beef in cans (known as 'bully beef') constituted the average soldier's daily fare. Food cooked on the frontline, when cooking was done at all, was carried out usually in just a couple of pots so that everything tasted of everything else. 'Seasoning' was provided by weeds or any other vegetation that came to hand, so that the hapless cooks soon took their place next to the military's top-brass on a soldier's hate list. If it hadn't been a punishable offence they might have pelted them with the uneaten loaves and stale biscuits which were invariably brick-hard before arriving in the trenches.

Passing thought might have been given by Seymour Mead to sending groceries to their uniformed employees in the war zones, especially in the days before food rationing was imposed: as it was, the only relief from the dismal fare served up to the troops came in food parcels from home. These continued to be sent throughout the duration of the war despite being misdirected, stolen, or simply unable to withstand the rigours of travel by military transport. *'I'm sorry if you sent any parcels,'* Sonny wrote to his mother during a spell in a field hospital, *'because they'll get lost while I'm in here.'* In a reference to how long it could take for a food parcel to reach him, he said in another letter *'...if you send any more [parcels] don't put any cheese in as it is very seldom good when it arrives.'* Perhaps it was the malodorous nature of some food parcels that provided the reason for the army to list them as being 'lost in transit.'

Sarah Boothroyd paid due heed to her son's advice, though like all women with men serving in the war getting together the makings of a food parcel became increasingly difficult as the shortages at home began biting deeper. Shops began closing early, their bare shelves replicas of the bare larders and kitchen tables belonging to their customers. There seemed never enough food to feed the rest of the family at Stanley Grove never mind Sonny in the trenches. Soon, there would be gloomier warnings of impending famine and although the government sat tight on the information for fear of encouraging the enemy, they knew there was barely two weeks supply of food left in the entire country. But somehow the food parcels to France and Flanders continued to flow. It seemed the increasingly deprived and undernourished families on the home front were becoming the mainstay of their wretched sons abroad.

Chapter 18

After being taken on by Seymour Mead in his early teens, Sonny earned his spurs as a delivery boy and general dogsbody before being elevated to the position of counter-assistant. Following that he became an indentured apprentice of the grocer's. Ahead of him lay seven, possibly eight, years of training and shop-floor experience before he'd be recognised as a fully qualified grocer. These years would be spent amidst canyons of canned soups and custard powder, the shelves stacked to the ceiling with tapioca, cornflakes, tinned beans and carrots, green peas, insect powder, nightlights and giant bottles of Lysol disinfectant. Working late into the evening would be expected, and as the shop doors closed another long shift opened. Blending tea, roasting coffee, stoning dried fruit, bottling beer and patting butter in preordained packages would be followed by restocking the shelves, bagging-up loose products, scrubbing counters and deciding how tomorrow's window display should be assembled. In winter, as the temperature dropped work continued on cold, often wet, tiled floors that led to various occupational ailments among older shop assistants, including chilblains, varicose veins and leg cramps.

However, for geography Sonny could not have made a better choice. His local Seymour Mead's occupied an entire corner at the junction of Stanley Grove and the Stockport Road with windows facing both busy thoroughfares. Sonny could have fallen out of bed and into his place of work quicker than it would have taken his eyes to blink open. There can be little doubt his mother, Sarah Boothroyd, was a regular customer at the store which may even have helped persuade the food retailer to employ Sonny. Before that could happen though, the boy had to go through a rigorous testing procedure to demonstrate he had the qualities necessary for working in a shop. Having clean fingernails and the means of providing a freshly laundered apron every day was the least of it: he also needed to show 'vitality' and a 'pleasing appearance' alongside the ability for showing deference to customers, especially the wealthier ones no matter how difficult and demanding they frequently were.

In joining the grocery chain, Sonny became part of a nationwide army of shop assistants who'd been the subject of much Parliamentary discourse around the turn of the twentieth century. Being spared the grimness of industrial work didn't mean shop assistants escaped being put upon despite being encouraged to see themselves as people of higher status. Behind the starched collars and obliging mannerisms lay long hours of labour and low pay. Rules that forbad them to sit down even when the shop was quiet went along with endless cycles of cleaning and tidying that took place in the intervals between delivering unimpeachable levels of customer service. For a grocer's assistant like Sonny the take home pay for all this scarcely exceeded that of a domestic servant – around £15 per annum.

The Shop Hours Act of 1892 limited working hours for young people in retail to a 'mere' 74 hours a week: and an added piece of legislation twelve years later gave local authorities the power to stipulate closing-times. One consequence of this remains something of an idiosyncrasy in some corners of Britain today – half-day closing, usually on a Wednesday. The English football club, Sheffield Wednesday, owes its name to the long-forgotten ordinance that enabled shop-workers time to engage with the game of soccer.

Although historians recall the Edwardian era as a time when the stays of Mother England were loosened, for the likes of Sonny Boothroyd profound inequality and class division continued being the principal features of the society they lived in. Few saw this as clearly as shop assistants. Sonny was a frontline observer of the disparity in wealth distribution because of the variety of customers coming through the door at Seymour Mead. First in usually were the overburdened housewives spreading their meagre budgets across the needs of a large family. They always bought in small quantities – loose products by the ounce, meat and fish by the halfpenny-worth. Even fuel for the fire was often bought avoirdupois. Though they continued buying from vendors in the street markets, multiple stores like Seymour Mead with their bulk buying policies and lower prices, were becoming a genuine alternative for working class families. At the time of the First World War one multiple grocery chain, Lipton's, had over 500 outlets across Britain making its proprietor an extremely wealthy man.

The next cohort to arrive at Mead's were the servant girls armed with shopping lists that Sonny had to copy out and deliver back to their mistresses in case something had been added at the foot for the maid's own personal consumption. Finally, in stepped the propertied panjandrums themselves, scions of the suburban rich who were not averse to commingling with the lower orders at the local multiple if it meant picking up a cheaper bottle of port or a cut-price side of pork. The fact they could buy on credit and have their bulk purchases rewarded with discounts, simply added to the appeal. As a shop worker, Sonny Boothroyd held the concession for looking through the windows of several disparate worlds during his spells behind the counter.

Although large numbers of shop assistants found work with small retailers, the shadow of the big high street stores continued to fall over everyone, their commercial power and influence keeping alive a culture that had changed little in the thirty-odd years leading up to the First World War. Around the time when Sonny's parents were being married, Debenham's for example, was saying this to their employees who through daily contact with wealthier customers might be tempted to get a little above themselves:

To Shop Assistants.

Any employee who is in the habit of…..
Smoking Spanish cigars.
Getting shaved in a barber's shop.
Going to dances and other such places of
　amusement.

Will surely give his employer reason to be suspicious of his INTEGRITY and all round HONESTY.

They also reminded staff that they were obliged to pay a contribution to the Church (one guinea a year), and attend Sunday School. After 14 hours work, Debenhams declared, *'spare time'* was to be devoted to *'reading good literature'*, though specific texts (perhaps the Bible was too obvious a choice to be quoted) were not identified. On a more generous note however, men were to be granted one evening a week for courting purposes, or two if they went to prayer meetings regularly. It was assumed that courting did not include taking the woman in your life to such dens of iniquity as the cinema or a variety theatre.

For Sonny Boothroyd and his colleagues these strict adherences were relaxed from time to time, although it would have required a finely tuned set of grocer's scales to measure the differences sometimes. Seymour Mead, in common with other like-minded employers, had a habit of hosting little soirees for their workers – tea-and-scones affairs - held in the local Conservative club with food supplied by the shop. Someone would play pianoforte, a girl would render a decorous song following which there was often a few games to enjoy. Ping-Pong was a favourite, though if you took on a senior member of the firm you had to be especially careful not to win.

It was all done not so much to encourage the modern idea of employee bonding as to demonstrate how caring and cordial the boss was despite what you might have garnered from the attitudes he displayed in the workplace. After delivering his lengthy, carefully prepared speech at the end of the soiree, a favoured employee would then respond by offering thanks and calling on those assembled to show their appreciation for the firm by working harder in the months to come. With the applause still ringing in his ears, the proprietor would be escorted to his waiting carriage (increasingly a chauffeur-driven motor vehicle), thoroughly convinced that in the eyes of his workers he wasn't such a bad fellow after all.

At 10 o'clock on Saturday nights Sonny would be at last free to forget work and enjoy what was left of the day with his chums. Often he'd avoid returning to 3 Stanley Grove first, choosing not to cross paths, or swords, with his father who'd be on the point of staggering home after several hours in the pub. Instead, after hanging up his apron and meeting his pals, they'd all make straight for what they considered to be the bright lights in their part of Manchester. Whatever distractions the Stockport Road had to offer – and by today's standards they didn't amount to much – it was fairly certain none of them included Debenham's idea of a night in with a good book.

Chapter 19

The soldier next to Sonny stares moodily down at the duckboards.

'If them that's keepin' this war going,' he says sullenly *'was to see what we 'ave to put up with, the buggers wouldn't stay longer than it takes me to scratch me arse.'*

Another soldier standing close-by nods vigorously, triggering a fit of coughing which earns him a rebuke from a passing corporal. *'Shut your noise!'* the officer snaps. *'Do you want to have us all on a charge?'* Even those struggling with the after-effects of battlefield gas are obliged to heed the 'whispers only' order as the enemy's line gets closer.

Another delay to the battalion's forward march is taking place, one of several that have plagued the unit since they left the road and entered the trench system. The trench guides are unsure about the safest way of continuing in territory whose devastation is devoid of any recognisable landmarks. The guides debate with each other and argue incessantly with the officers in charge of the relief operation, making little effort to conceal their differences from the men. By this point in the war so many of the battalion's original officers have been killed or wounded, it's been necessary to fill the gaps with less-experienced men, many of them until recently still serving in the ranks. Their training has been brief and rudimentary, very different from what their predecessors received earlier in the conflict. At the Army School of Instruction the first cohorts of officer material had been taught to inspire confidence and comradeship in their units, fostering what was called 'a soldierly spirit' in the men under their command. Now, at the end of 1917, it's left largely to the men themselves to develop such virtues.

In an army, which according to Lloyd George himself, has been *'scraped-up'* from men previously working in low-grade occupations or rejected on the grounds of being unfit for military service, an entirely different set of problems in man-management has arisen and many of the new breed of officers don't have the skills, the time or the patience to cope with them. Gone are the enthusiastic young volunteers of the PALS who'd marched off to war as if it was some sort of glorious game: in their places are conscripts hastened into action and coarsened by being spattered with the blood and brains of their fellow soldiers.

It is a situation which tests a soldier's loyalties and encourages the nullifying bitterness that rests at the heart of the blame culture. Everybody from the top brass down gets it in the neck: but because senior commanders keep themselves comfortably out of the main combat zones, it is the officers on the battlegrounds who attract most of the flak. How they begrudge the liberties given to the men they've replaced - those university and public school types, who at the outbreak of war were given the time and facilities for developing as officers with the added luxury of being allowed to take their servants with them to training camp.

While the arguments continue, at least the 'other ranks' can now fall-out and take a breather. Sonny drops his haversack to the ground and sits on it, knees drawn up to his chest. The mood of the trenches is often as unpredictable as the taste of army food. From being dreary and depressing it can suddenly lighten, often with flashes of macabre humour. A soldier tells of a burial party he was detailed to recently where they'd no sooner dug the grave than the Germans started shelling them. The burial party dived into the hole for protection leaving the corpse still lying on the surface. When the bombardment was over they resurface unscathed. *'We was like coffin-cases ourselves,'* the soldier laughs, *'rising from the ground like it was Judgement Day. The only thing waitin' for us was this dead bloke showing no signs whatever of comin' back to fuckin' life!'*

Much current trench talk consists of swapping stories about wild hand-to-hand fighting with the enemy, something Sonny's battalion experienced as recently as October when a Company H.Q. was raided by a bombing party of around 20 Germans. The raiders had approached undetected from across no-man's land and reached the Company's dugout whereupon mayhem ensued. The Manchesters fought back with anything that came to hand – rifle butts, self-styled wooden clubs, even their bare knuckles were brought into action. Eventually, an officer brandishing his pistol saw the raiding party off but not before five of his unit had been wounded.

Soon, talk switches to the pros and cons of the battalion's deployment once the relief has been completed. The fire step of the frontline trenches will be home to some of them, the supply trenches behind providing rough shelter for the others. Either way soldiers will have to endure not just mud and water but also the stench - an amalgam of battlefield waste and the all-pervading stink of lime chloride, the liquid compound applied to just about everything in the hope of reducing infection and disease. And as if that wasn't enough, there are the latrines to contend with.

The latrines in the combat areas are usually so vile a soldier will avoid using them if he can. As if to underline the point, a man further along the duckboards from Sonny takes a pre-emptive pee into an empty bully beef can before hiking it over the trench parapet. It's something Sonny has witnessed before, including once where a man used a spiked German helmet (the Pickelhaube) to urinate in. The helmet, taken as a trophy from a German corpse, was used in this fashion as a way of showing contempt for those on the other side of the wire entanglements.

Now Sonny tips his own helmet forward so he can lean back against the trench wall and rest his eyes for a moment or two. If the officers up ahead are unsure about how to continue with what is regarded as a standard manoeuvre, it is nothing compared to the uncertainty felt by their men about how the war is progressing as a whole. The only thing beyond doubt at the end of 1917 is that the troops are being fed less information about the conduct of the war than they received when first arriving in France. Facts about progress on the war front, like food on the home front, are subject to increasing levels of rationing.

They've heard that the armies of their Russian allies have disintegrated and long since departed for home, although the reason for this, to add their weight to the Bolshevik revolution, hasn't registered with the British as being an event destined to shake the world. The French too have mutinied, upwards of half-a-million men holding their officers at gunpoint, electing soldiers councils and singing songs of liberation as they headed for Paris. *'We are not so stupid,'* they'd chanted at their commanders *'as to march against undamaged machine guns!'*

There are rumours also of unrest among Australian troops, and it is now a fact that the Italians have decided to pack their troubles in their old kit bags and return home to their wives and children. Only the British Tommy seems prepared to fight on, doggedly splashing through mud and water, obediently doing his duty long after it's become questionable not so much what his duty is, but where it's likely to lead him and to what ultimate effect. To victory over the enemy is the stock answer, though no poll would be needed to show how massively the troops would respond to any proposal aimed at ending the war, or even bringing about a suspension to hostilities. What registers more is the seemingly inviolable belief that the war they are fighting is the war to end all wars...the only way to establishing an honourable and permanent peace. It's a strong message difficult to dislodge in the minds of these 'civilians in khaki.' As they've been taught to see it, Britain is a nation that considers itself the civilising force in a barbaric world, the race ordained to bring the values of the British way of life to those unable or unwilling to develop them for themselves. *'What made you join-up in the first place?'* Sonny had heard one of his comrades asked. *'They talked me into it,'* was the reply. *'My family, the newspapers, people I trusted...and my own vanity of course. They made a big thing of it, being proud to serve your country and what it stands for.'*

Among the enemy's soldiers, the story is not quite the same. Through diplomatic channels, Germany has sued for peace – a move that goes some way towards recognising the disillusionment and low-morale of their soldiers on the battlefields. *'Life here isn't worth a damn,'* wrote Fritz Meese, a private in the German army, *'and one thinks nothing of losing it.'* Later, he added, *'Today I walked for half-an-hour through violent rifle fire just to have a wash and because I hoped to get one or two cigarettes.'* It was as if what was being fought over had become less and less important to those doing the fighting. Nevertheless, the Allies rejected any idea of a truce and Germany's offer of talks on the matter became another casualty of the war.

Sonny now levers himself stiffly to his feet and thuds his boots quietly on the trench boards. Beyond thoughts of the battalion's next return to base camp, his mind goes back to the things a soldier often clings to in times of danger. Brief, disjointed images fill his head – the enviable warmth at this time of the year inside the kitchen at Stanley Grove: the tramcars lurching their way along the Stockport Road: and locking the doors of Seymour Mead's leaving him free at last to join his chums. Where these chums are now, Sonny has little way of knowing. Conscripted no doubt, serving in the trenches, some maybe not so far from where he is now waiting for the march to resume. He prays none of them have been killed and that when this horror is over they'll all get back together again....

The 'Old Lie.'

The poet Wilfred Owen saw active service in the war with Sonny's Manchester Regiment. At one point he was detailed to go through the content of soldier's letters. 'I have censored hundreds of them today,' he said, 'and the hope for peace is in every one.' Owens's most-quoted poem about the war indicts those who peddled the 'old lie' that it is 'sweet and decorous' to die for your country. After returning to the battlegrounds from a psychiatric hospital he was fatally wounded a week before the Armistice was signed.

Chapter 20

'Well mother...' Sonny wrote in April 1917, *'we keep going over and having a scrap with the Bosch, and up to now I have had the luck to come through safe. As you say keep on smiling and the day will come when we will have the cause to smile.'*

His letter, containing its guileless expressions of hope, was posted from the trenches during a pause in the battles around Arras - battles that had begun a few weeks earlier in flurries of snow carried on the back of gale force winds. Arras started on an Easter Monday, a day when rocks reputedly gave way to resurrection, and death gave way to eternal life. At Arras, however, the message was drowned in the fury of artillery barrages and life only too easily gave way to its antithesis.

Douglas Haig had never meant Arras to be anything other than a deception, a feint to draw the Germans away from another section of the Western Front where French forces were set to attack them on the Hindenburg Line but the Germans were not to be fooled. They cut the French to tatters and although suffering heavy losses caused enough chaos amongst the British to vindicate their policy of fighting a defensive war and letting their enemy exhaust itself in meaningless, unfruitful attacks. Haig knew Arras would never succeed, but declared it an offensive deemed necessary for the *'greater strategic good.'* What this meant exactly had more than a few of his generals scratching their heads: but it mattered little especially to the newspapers back home. The six miles of ground gained at Arras together with the number of prisoners taken and the amount of German armaments captured was seen as enough to declare the venture *'another great Allied success.'*

On the first day of the battle at Arras, Billy Bishop of the Royal Flying Corps, circling above the trenches described what he saw from the cockpit of his aircraft:

'Suddenly over the top of our parapets a thin line of infantry crawled up and commenced to stroll casually toward the enemy. To me it seemed that they must soon wake up and run: that they were altogether too slow: that they could not realise the great danger they were in. Here and there a shell would burst as the line advanced or halted for a moment. Three of four men near the burst would topple over like so many tin soldiers. Two or three other men would then come running up to the spot from the rear with a stretcher, pick up the wounded and the dying and slowly walk back with them. I could not get the idea out of my head that it was just a game they were playing: it all seemed so unreal. I could not make myself realise the full truth or meaning of it all. It seemed I was from an entirely different world, looking down from another sphere on this strange, uncanny puppet-show.'

Among the 'tin soldiers' were units of the Manchester Regiment, including Sonny Boothroyd's 19th battalion. They went over the top together and fought for the next three weeks at great cost in life and limb. By April 27th every unit except Sonny's had suffered over a hundred dead or wounded. Worse still was the fate of other battalions fighting alongside. The Royal Scots Fusiliers were entirely wiped out, their commanding officer killed and all other officers killed or wounded. In the chaos surrounding an attack on the village of Cherisy, this is how the 19th battalion's Lieutenant-Colonel Whitehead described events:

'At 6.00 p.m. the attack was launched and the result was very much as I had expected. The frontage was too wide for companies to keep in touch and an entry into the enemy trench was (only) effected at isolated points. During the advance a good many casualties were suffered from our own barrage. When the men came under machine-gun fire they doubled forward and the officers and sergeants were unable in the noise and excitement to hold them back. A and B companies were able to join up in the German front line. The trench was still full of enemy and there was no sign of the battalion who I had been told were to do the mopping-up. Heavy machine gun fire was coming from the enemy second line trench. As A company was by this time reduced to about nineteen men and B company to about sixteen men, it was impossible to advance further without leaving behind them an un-mopped trench full of enemy. All the officers of both companies had become casualties and the NCOs in charge decided to hang on to what they had won....'

Throughout the hours of darkness the scattered soldiers of Sonny's unit held on until men of another regiment were mustered to support them. By April 29th the total casualties suffered by the 19th battalion was around 1,000 men – almost two-thirds of the overall casualties suffered by the entire army Division of which they were part. It left the Division's commander-in-chief, Sir John Shea, little choice but to resign from his post.

Writing to a fellow officer a few days after the carnage, Wilfrith Elstob, a Lieutenant in the Manchester Regiment, reflected on the losses adding how soldiers in war often had a greater grasp of the truth than those who affect to know more about such matters:

'I hardly dare mention the losses for my heart is full and I know how you will feel. On the battlefield as one moved between shells and bullets, death seemed a very small thing and at times enviable. Here we are, English and German..we, or rather those damned journalists talk about hate..it seems to me to disappear on the battlefield, people who have not been there talk a lot of damned nonsense. We are 'blind' as a private soldier on the night after the battle said to me. 'We know it is not their quarrel, sir,' this spontaneously. Our fellows...it's always cigarettes or hot tea or something like that when they take prisoners, and the Germans fed and kept alive our fellows in the midst of the bitterest fighting last year. Thank God! Humanity and unselfishness are higher than a damned lot of talked nonsense by certain petty minded people.'

Elstob, a man with a mind more like a human being's than a senior army officer, was to be killed in the last year of the war at the Battle of St Quentin. chillingly in the vicinity of a redoubt called 'Manchester Hill.'

Elsewhere on the Western Front, Allied troops were demonstrating their disenchantment with Arras in other ways. In the Champagne area Sengalese units of the French colonial army had deserted their positions and fled, boarding hospital trains as a way of speeding their departure to safety at the rear. Shortly afterwards, mutinies amongst other French infantry battalions had spread to no less than sixteen army corps. The red flag rather than the regimental one was raised, and a list of soldier's demands were presented before they'd agree to go back into combat. Even when they did they made it clear that...*'We will defend the trenches, but not attack.'* One regiment that did agree eventually to man the frontline marched-in famously baa-ing like sheep - animals driven to the slaughter. For the remainder of 1917 the French army ceased to be a reckonable force in the First World War.

As the battle-worn men of Sonny Boothroyd's 19th battalion were finally able to withdraw from the Arras area, it might have been said that many of them had the appearance of animals themselves...wild, terrified animals with eyes deadened by the atrocities they'd been forced to witness. Further along the line, however, others of the Manchester Regiment fought on...at Bullecourt, for example, where they were almost ritualistically slaughtered for Douglas Haig's 'greater good.' Now they understood - these civilians in khaki, these young men who in their workplaces were growing accustomed to innovation and technology - how far behind the military were in the industrialisation of war. The German machine gun ruled, its power greater than the Kaiser could ever have dreamt of. *'We are not so stupid as to march against machine guns,'* the French soldiers had declared, although unlike their British counterparts, they were not an army raised from the city's urbanised middle class and conscripted factory workers, but mostly from the peasantry.

The smell of cordite, the all-enveloping gas clouds, the sweat and body fluids of fear and desperation...like camp followers, the stench of war was forever present no matter what distance soldiers put between themselves and the frontline trenches. But Sonny Boothroyd was one tin soldier who'd survived, even if Arras was merely a few strides closer to even bigger events to come. At some point along the route he was now about to travel, the 3rd Battle of Ypres...forever afterwards known as Passenchaendale...awaited him.

Chapter 21

Sitting in Downing Street as Arras floundered to a finish was David Lloyd George, Britain's recently appointed prime minister and head of the country's wartime coalition government. He was also adjudged to be Douglas Haig's fiercest critic, although his disapproval of the man didn't bring about much in the way of changing the field-marshall's rigid mindset as to how the war was to be fought. The prime minister may have bowled his commander-in-chief a few bouncers in the latter-half of the conflict, but Haig survived unscathed to complete his innings. On the Western Front the shedding of blood would continue uninterrupted.

Historians have found it convenient to depict the conflict between Haig and Lloyd George as being rooted in their personalities or the factors driving their personal ambitions. Haig possibly dreamt of achieving Napoleon-like eminence after crushing the enemy: and Lloyd George wouldn't have been the career politician he was if he hadn't fretted over the damage high casualty rates were doing to his reputation and his chances of winning the next Parliamentary election but beyond that both shared a common goal - to put Germany to the sword as a means of eliminating them as a rival power in the world. In that sense their frequent spats amounted to no more than how this was to be accomplished, and any idea that the prime minister was at serious odds with Haig and his disregard for the lives of his troops, is really beside the point and becomes more ludicrous the more it is repeated. Both men had their feet planted firmly in the soil that had grown the British Empire.

Lloyd George's rather weak alternative to the continuing carnage on the battlegrounds of the Western Front was to propose opening an offensive on the Italian Front, so drawing away some of Germany's firepower on Haig's area of operations. To achieve this would have meant transferring some of the commander-in-chief's army divisions to Italy, in so doing casting serious doubt on Haig's perennial belief that the Germans were on the point of collapse and open to being routed. To Haig, Lloyd George's proposal was equal to saying he had failed as a military commander, that his strategy was wrong-headed, and the outcome of the war would be decided by generals elsewhere outside of his control. Haig was appalled and deeply offended by the proposal, at times incensed by it. Even his old friend, King George the Fifth, seemed incapable or unwilling to come to his aid: and just as news of one brief triumph for the British at Messines was filtering through to London, the Chief of the Imperial General Staff, Sir William Robertson, was writing to Haig:

'There is trouble in the land just now...the Lloyd George idea is to settle the war from Italy, and today the railway people have been asked for figures regarding the rapid transfer of 12 Divisions and 300 heavy guns to Italy. They will never go while I am C.I.G.S. but that will

come later. What I want to impress on you is:- Don't argue that you can finish the war this year, or that the German is already beaten. Argue that your plan is the best plan...that no other would be safe let alone decisive, and leave them to reject your advice and mine. They dare not do that.'

It was clear to Haig from this note that Robertson too was not altogether unwavering in his support for him. Indeed, Robertson later hinted he might be interested in trying out the prime minister's Italy idea, especially if the continuing casualty figures indicated that by later in 1917 Britain could be a whisker close to having an under-strength army. Haig's moodiness and resentment for the prime minister was now added to by his disappointment with Robertson.

Whatever feelings Lloyd George had for Haig (many of which he released publicly only after the war was over) he was never to act on them with any great vigour. Consequently, the stand-off between them has probably been made too much off down the decades. A photograph of the two men meeting al fresco behind the battle lines at one point in 1917 has often been used to underpin the notion that an unbridgeable gap existed in their approach to winning the war. It shows an unusually animated Haig leaning towards the prime minister making a 'let-me-tell-you-something' gesture with his hand while Lloyd George, looking in need of a barber, stands squarely on his polished shoes looking quite unimpressed but the rift (and surely the two were far from agreement in terms of the reasons for the huge casualty figures) has been made into something like a clash of ideologies, which it certainly was not. The war on the Western Front continued to take its toll of human flesh, and no one of significance resigned on principle or was removed from their post. There may have been dark mutterings in the corridors of power, but that was as far as it went. Even the dispute over the Italian Front was resolved by sending just a few token divisions there from Flanders.

Added to the question of Lloyd George's resolve and sincerity over the number of young men perishing on the battlegrounds, is the not entirely unrelated matter of who he appointed to his inner war cabinet. For a former pacifist and ardent social reformer he seemed to have collected around him a strange retinue of people who most of us would think had little empathy for what the Liberal prime minister wanted to achieve.

The first of these was the Leader of the House of Lords, Lord Curzon, an Eton and Oxford educated Conservative who'd been appointed Viceroy of India at the height of Britain's land-grabbing activities on the subcontinent. He'd grabbed the North-West Frontier and also presided over the partition of Bengal, something he'd carried out in such brutal fashion that even Kitchener (heavens forbid!) complained about it, helping in the end to have Curzon's orders revoked.

As an M.P. Curzon had also been so bitterly opposed to women being given the vote, that he'd taken charge of the Anti-Suffrage League, relinquishing it only when Humphry Ward and her White Feather brigade came along. In private life he'd married an American millionairess, and his daughter was later to marry the British fascist leader, Oswald Mosely. Ironically, Curzon's self-proclaimed talent for monumental sculpture led him to designing the original Whitehall Cenotaph – the site for Remembrance Day services ever since.

Also taking his place in Lloyd George's war cabinet was another peer of the realm, Lord Milner, a former colonial administrator whose domineering attitude towards the Boers after the annexation of the Transvaal and Orange Free State had been the trigger for the Boer War. He'd insisted that children in the newly-grabbed South African colonies were taught in English irrespective of their origins, and brought in a small regiment of lesser-lights (subsequently known as 'Milner's Kindergarten') to administer his autocratic decrees – one of these acolytes being the author of many an Empire-inspired adventure story, John Buchan. On returning to Britain, Milner continued espousing his right-wing views by taking his seat in the House of Lords and was appointed to the war cabinet a few days after the First World War began. It came as no surprise to friends and foes alike that he later led the call for armed intervention against the USSR after the Bolsheviks took control there in 1917.

But if Milner and Curzon's views ran predictably within the lines of their land grabbing instincts, what was to be made of another war cabinet appointment, Arthur Henderson, leader of the Labour Party after the resignation of Ramsey MacDonald? Here was a man of working-class stock who'd begun life in a Glasgow locomotive factory at the age of 12 and as a union leader had been to the fore in the struggles of the Iron Founders Union. For several years he had been their full-time paid organiser. After a religious conversion, however, he became a lay preacher and his views changed radically. He now opposed any move to federate unions which would have increased their bargaining power, and became virulently anti-strike. After entering the House of

Commons he attracted the notice of Lloyd George who, when he became prime minister, immediately nodded him through to his seat on the war cabinet.

Henderson's appointment to the inner-sanctum of decision making in the First World War was another example of Lloyd George's adroitness at side-stepping any threat to his plans - in this case from the organised workers of Britain. By selecting someone who appeared to be 'one of their own' he sought to pre-empt any widespread opposition to the war and, following the introduction of conscription, keep the armed services replete with men drawn from the mass of Britain's manual workers. In many ways he set a benchmark for succeeding generations of political leaders only too willing to indulge in the sham of running what they hoped they could sell as a 'balanced' administration.

The decision to put the South African Jan Smuts in the war cabinet, however, must have struck many observers as little short of bizarre. As old soldier himself Smuts might have been regarded as a suitable choice for helping decide the course of a war: his soldiering, however, had been as a guerrilla leader with the Boers during the South African war. He'd led commando raids against British troops and had been a member of the Boer government leading up to Kitchener's attempted genocide. He'd written extensively against the British occupation of the Boer states, and whatever claims he was later to make that the best thing for the world was '...the extension of the ideas that have produced the British Commonwealth', he was nevertheless guilty of killing British soldiers. Switching allegiances, however, like selling armaments to both sides in a conflict, wasn't entirely unknown amongst those seeking to fulfil their political ambitions, and Smuts was not the first to do so. His speeches, delivered in a characteristically high-pitched tone, impressed many senior Westminster figures including Winston Churchill who wanted Smuts to be given the title of honorary field marshall of the British army. What Douglas Haig made of this proposal was never recorded for posterity.

Such then was the composition of the war cabinet: an inner-circle of a larger grouping called the War Committee, who was kept as much in the dark as to what was being planned for the First World War battlefields as the families of soldiers serving there. The personnel of this inner-circle changed marginally from time to time, Milner being replaced in the Spring of 1918 and Henderson giving way to George Barnes who was also a member of Lloyd George's coalition government. Barnes refused to resign when the Labour Party belatedly withdrew its support for the coalition and the war in 1918. In doing so he felt justified in continuing to draw a government minister's salary for a further two-and-a-half years.

If Lloyd George ever thought seriously of forcing Douglas Haig to relinquish his command or even consider substantial changes to his conduct of the war, then he would have found it well nigh impossible to get the endorsement of those around him in the war cabinet. It would have been the equivalent of asking turkeys to vote for Christmas. The majority vote of the inner-circle would have been a resounding 'No!' and consequently any fulminating by the prime minister with respect to his commander-in-chief was carried on in private and written about long afterwards. Haig was free to carry on regardless. And carry on he did, burying the tragedies of the Somme, Arras and other fruitless campaigns in order to concentrate on an even more reckless affair. In London Lloyd George may well have held his head in his hands as reports reached him of further stupendous losses on the Western Front. On the Western Front itself, however, Haig's mind was set on other things. The Third Battle of Ypres... Paschendaele...had now moved to the forefront of his mind.

Chapter 22

There are times when Sonny could be persuaded that swapping stories of a prurient nature has become mandatory in the trenches. Soldiers seldom tire of discussing sex and when circumstances permit will break into song about it. One song, 'The Ball of Kirriemuir', has an appeal wider than the Western Front itself. It describes in graphic detail what takes place after a rather dignified soiree degenerates into a sexual free-for-all in which everyone from the grand lady of the house to the humblest domestic servant has a role in the orgy that develops. Sonny reckons 'Kirriemuir' must have around 100 verses with more being added all the time: it's that kind of song, growing in proportion to the febrile imaginings of men denied a comfortable bed containing consenting female company.

For most soldiers, however, sex is only to be had well behind the lines where amongst the towns and villages as yet un-shattered by war, certain sections of what is known as 'camp followers' transact their shadowy, and at times, not un-lucrative trade. Camp followers as a whole have been a feature of land armies ever since men first took up arms against other men, and in the First World War women working as prostitutes are just part of a motley collection of individuals that include wide-boys and racketeers, cheap booze and tobacco merchants, holy willies and religious freaks, and of course plenty of quack doctors whose living depends on searching out those damaged by war and persuading them to purchase their fake remedies. Over-dutiful servants are also to be found in the ranks of the camp followers, the liegemen and lackeys of commissioned officers, still bent on providing the personal support services their uniformed master's were accustomed to receiving before joining the military.

Standing somewhat aloof, however, and hoping to maintain a dignified distance between themselves and the others are the carpetbaggers - salesmen usually, working for military equipment contractors and smaller, lesser-known weapons companies. In their cheap business suits and felt hats, they strike an odd note scurrying around the tented encampments looking to intercept military personnel who they believe might have an authorised budget to spend. They also do business with individual soldiers, men whose weapons have been lost or stolen, or simply disabled by the mud and water surrounding them in the trenches.

But it's the prostitutes who constitute anything like a collective – a group containing more than a few wretched and abandoned females selling the only asset they have left…themselves. On pay-day queues form outside their shared premises, something the military brass either tolerate or else choose to ignore for most of the time. Their officers, after all, are not unacquainted with such places even if their visits are prearranged privately through pimps and other contacts in the local sex industry. The only thing an officer has to be mindful of is to enter a brothel showing a blue light rather than a red one above the door. Blue is for officers, a red light indicates an establishment for the use of 'other ranks' only. Neither foot soldiers nor their commanding officers, however, will think anything of making a long journey by any available means of transport in order to spend a few fleeting moments of forgetfulness in the calculated embrace of a complete stranger. In 1917 the going rate is £1 for one half-hour's pleasure. Often the 'pleasure' lasts considerably shorter than that, although the price by all accounts seems always to stay the same.

In the frequent, short delays that now bedevil the 19th battalion's progress to the frontline, Sonny has time to eavesdrop on some of the conversations taking place around him, talk that inevitably turns towards his fellow-infantryman's experiences with women. There seems almost to be a correlation between the growing sense of danger and the need soldiers have to talk about sex. It's as if the possibility of imminent death finds a conduit for escape in discussing the act that provides the overture to life. Now that home leave is becoming a rarity, a soldier's imagination takes over so that previous sex encounters are enlarged and embroidered with so much fantasy that it becomes impossible to tell what's true and what's being made up. In the context of what men have come to endure in this war, it is self-censorship dispensed with… overruled…thrown to the rats.

A man produces some sepia photographs, dog-eared and dirty, of a sex scene which he magnanimously passes around. Other soldiers nearby giraffe their necks to have a squint at them in the fading light. Some men, however, glance away, not so much in disgust as anxiety. In the municipalities of the camp followers' brothels, diseases are acquired which nothing will budge, sexually transmitted diseases that in the absence of antibiotics the victim will carry with him like amputated toes or a shrapnel wound for the rest of his days. Fifteen minutes with Venus, they've heard it said, followed by umpteen years with Mercury – mercury being the prescribed treatment, and about the only hope a man has, of coping with venereal disease.

The word is that some female camp followers are so disease-ridden, the military view them as constituting a threat to the army's morale and discipline, and thereby a threat also to a man's effectiveness in battle. Rounding them up from time to time, often on the pretext of their being infiltrators and spies, the antidote to the problem is either to deport them or else have them shot. Like some of their former clients branded as 'deserters', the last thing these hapless women will see is the blindfold's dark shape moving in against the hues of rising dawn.

Around Sonny, other pictures are now being unearthed – photographs of wives and fiancées, girlfriends and sisters, female cousins and groups of women photographed in the workplace. All overt references to sex now vanish, replaced by much acclaim for the beauties smiling out from the celluloid. The men in possession of these prints stand proudly by, regarding themselves as the subject of envy and admiration in those around them. No one cares to suggest that getting your photograph taken involves much preening and grooming beforehand, so that the finished item is invariably far from how their paramours look most of the time. To every man this is how the women in their lives look...in their eyes, how they will always look. Before putting the pictures away their owners give them a last lingering look. Who knows when this bloody war will be over and girls return to being the one major item on a young man's personal agenda. The demure looks and fixed smiles of the photographs will hopefully one day give way to eyes hinting at more than the camera is capable of revealing. For the time being, however, a soldier must rely solely on his memories…and his imagination.

   Sonny circles his arms in the air trying to squeeze out the stiffness, but succeeds only in restoring the pain of the shrapnel wound to his shoulder. When a snow cloud engulfs the moon the darkness around him is all but complete. Even at close range, looking at a soldier's personal belongings has now become virtually impossible. He wonders if a parcel or a couple of letters will be waiting for him when this stint on the frontline is finished. A few weeks ago he had written to Stanley Grove after coming out of the trenches complaining of having a vicious cold which only added to his mood of depression. 'I will be glad when it's all over,' he said. 'Lads that go on leave now are lucky to get fourteen days. Next leave I hope is the last with the army.' Following this he wrote again: 'I am just thinking of chucking this job…giving in a week's notice.' If the military's morale-measurers were listening they were surely in no doubt how Sonny and his comrades now felt about a war that seemed to have no end. At any rate, for once his comments were allowed to pass, uncensored.

   As the delays continue frustration builds within the men of the 19th battalion. No one wants to see the frontline trenches sooner than necessary: but few things are worse than being stuck in the penetrating cold. A sudden flurry of snow descends on the duckboards, freezing over as it lands, turning the wooden slats white and treacherous. Thoughts turn to the work they'll be detailed for throughout the night, then after daybreak the prospects of some warm food and a little shut-eye. Enclosed by the damp walls of a dugout, they will make themselves as comfortable as possible and try forgetting the war for a while. They might even be able to ignore the rats if they're lucky. Before falling into un-refreshing slumber, however, thoughts of home and the women they've known will return to engage their thoughts. Perhaps this will trigger a little localised sensation that will be dealt with under cover of a blanket once those around them are adjudged to have fallen asleep.

As sex goes, that's about all that can be managed for the moment………

Chapter 23

Touring their dominion of shops spread across Lancashire must have been a de-vitalising experience for Seymour Mead as the German blockade of major English ports continued and stocks of basic foodstuffs dwindled even further. Having pushed, prodded and cajoled over three hundred employees into volunteering for the First World War, the whole thing now looked like becoming an albatross around their neck. While other businesses were launching themselves anew on the wings of wartime contracts awarded by government, Seymour Mead was being forced to make do with humbler fare. How they must have envied some of Manchester's other merchants who appeared to be coining it in.

Thomas Duerr, for example, had been asked early in the war to make provision for supplying the British army with jam. The troops in the trenches consumed jam in prodigious quantities intent on achieving the 'sugar rush' it was capable of producing. At the time however, because there was little in the way of comprehensive food standards in place, fillers such as wood chips and talcum powder were often added to products like jam. Soldiers complained so much and so consistently about this that the government decided to invite Duerr's to provide something more like the real thing, which they duly did from their Old Trafford factory in Manchester, establishing a reputation for quality that continues to the present day.

However, Duerr was just one of several suppliers to the military who found themselves striking it lucky as the war continued. The pharmacy chain Boots began producing tablets for purifying water – something of inestimable value to soldiers on the battlegrounds where wholesome drinking water was often at a premium. Boots manufactured approximately 115 million tablets in record time before going on to provide the chemicals for respirators that helped mitigate the effects of inhaling battlefield gas. It could be said the pharmacist's contract from government went far in breathing fresh life into the company.

Other retailers, many of them in the clothing industry, were also busy using their connections with the military to brighten their commercial horizons. Acquascutum for instance made trench coats for First World War army officers as well as coats for sailors, airmen's jackets and other forms of protective clothing. These sat alongside the range of more-fashionable attire that Acquascutum was famous for selling to the great and the good in society, many of them long standing customers of the firm. Burberry's were similarly involved although they actually designed an entirely new army officer's uniform and had Lord Kitchener and other generals as their clients. Gieves & Hawkes, who'd once boasted Lord Nelson as a client and went on to become the primary source of advice to the wealthy on correct and proper ways of dressing, used their links with the Royal Naval

College to supply sailor's uniforms: and through a mini-cartelisation process they soon cornered the market in cap badges and gold braid. More germane to the circumstances of those fighting the First World War at sea however, was their development of an inflatable lifebelt.

One of the more intriguing ventures for moneymaking in the war was that entered into by Aspreys - today the provider of luxury goods to Arab princes and former ruling heads of Europe. They created a separate military department at the time of the First World War supplying camping equipment to the army. Instead of mounting a rather grand exhibition of their products at their London showrooms however, they sent their staff out to flog tents at various army-training camps around England. Rolling out the red carpet for their wealthier clients was temporarily suspended while their salesmen splashed around in the mud at places like Salisbury Plain.

Whatever the retailers managed to rake in from their efforts, it was small beer compared to what the munitions manufacturers were making from their products. Such was the demand for shells and other explosives the munitions makers introduced round-the-clock working at their factories. Workers in their thousands, many of them women, donned their dungarees and became part of the swelling army of civilians making the armaments their husbands, sons and relations would fire during the First World War. In several parts of the country state-owned ordinance factories sprang up to help supply the needed ammunition.

In private sector munitions, the Birmingham Small Arms Company (BSA) had always been an arms manufacturer, although in the early 1900s their reputation rested more on making pedal bikes and motorcycles. The First World War however, brought a bounty in weapons production and they began supplying Lewis guns, shells and military vehicles. Further north the Armstrong Group of companies made munitions and built warships: and at Billingham on Teesside synthetic ammonia for bomb-making was the mainstay of the areas economy. From Clydeside to Jarrow, from Tyneside to Barrow-in-Furness naval yards were also in full production.

Connected to shipping were Barr & Stroud, a firm adopted by the navy who contracted them to provide rangefinders and optical instruments for use in war. Shrewdly they appointed Sir W.G. Armstrong Mitchell (he of the Armstrong Group) as their sales agent abroad, which did their turnover no harm at all. In 1914 the firm made over £1 million in sales (a record in the history of the company), half of it from the Admiralty and War Office contracts, the rest from overseas. At First World War prices this was quite an accomplishment, and enabled Barr & Stroud to employ over a thousand highly skilled workers at their plants.

On an individual level Frederick Wilfred Stokes grew a small fortune from inventing the Stokes mortar – a standard piece of artillery on the battlefields of First World War Europe. Chairman and Managing Director of a crane making plant in Ipswich, Stokes had been obsessed for much of his life with refining the technology of warfare and producing more effective weaponry. Before he died he got his reward: his mortar was regarded as indispensable by the military, and he was given a knighthood by a grateful government.

More sinister by far though, were the mighty arms dealers and manufacturers who bestrode both sides in the conflict that took Sonny Boothroyd from Manchester to the mayhem of the Western Front. Thyssens, the biggest competitor to the giant Krupp empire in Germany, mined iron ore for use by both French and German steelmakers in the First World War. Krupp was at the time the biggest industrial company in the world, 50 per cent of its output being in armaments. Two years before the outbreak of war they'd sold warships to the Kaiser and did similar business with 32 other governments in the world. Wherever a war was taking place Krupp, they said, would always be there beating off the competition. During the First World War they found it highly profitable selling arms to both the Central Powers and the Allies. Later, Krupp was to become the main source of supplying arms to Adolf Hitler, and one of the Krupp family, Alfred, was convicted as a war criminal at Nuremberg.

Out of the same mould came another individual, Basil Zaharoff, who'd later become known as 'The Merchant of Death.' Reputed to have had holdings in Krupp and other munitions companies, Zaharoff made himself a multimillionaire by selling arms to both the Boers and the British during the South African wars. He was Chairman of the U.K. firm Vickers-Armstrong at the time. Described as the 'mystery man' of Europe, there wasn't much in what he did that required the services of a sleuth to uncover. He simply fostered warfare, networking with senior European politicians including Lloyd George, using the knowledge gained in one place to alarm those in another, and subsequently persuading them to prepare for conflict by buying arms through his agency. Shrugging off criticism of his role in fomenting strife, he persisted in imaging himself as a modern businessman doing what all businessmen do – responding to the needs of the market. It was as if he was just encouraging people to keep their clothes clean by selling them washing powder. Despite the criticism, however, and the sinister aura surrounding him Zaharoff was in the end to be decorated by the French and granted a knighthood by the British.

It would have surprised no one if Zaharoff had been shown to have had connections with the munitions industry in the United States during the First World War. People like him traded worldwide, an early example of what is now called the global economy. The fact that globalisation arose from death and destruction mattered little to the American giants whose business was in the international munitions markets. During the period of American 'neutrality' in the First World War, they still managed to send over $2 billion worth of war supplies to the Allies. In the process they created 21,000 new millionaires. Firms like Du Ponts, Bethlehem Steel, United States Steel, Utah Copper and the General Chemical Company all saw their income multiply through servicing a war their government steadfastly refused to be involved with until it was more than half way over.

American aircraft manufacturers and those who supplied the engines did equally well commercially, even better if you consider none of their products ever left the ground and not a single plane made it to the European war zones. They at least could argue, however feebly, they didn't have a hand in turning blood into gold. Unlike the others who made their fortunes from the First World War and other wars to follow, the aircraft makers were allowed the luxury of denial.

Chapter 24

In June 1917, soon after the Manchester's had finished fighting around the area of Arras, Sonny wrote, '*Well mother, we are preparing for another attack soon which we all like...I don't think!*' In the same letter, he added '*I would rather be attacking the manager at Seymour Mead's than the Bosche.*'

The 'attack' he alluded to had already been officially designated by the military as the 3rd Battle of Ypres, although to everyone thereafter it was to be better known as 'Passchendaele' – the name of a small town near Ypres which was eventually to become synonymous with all the futility that had characterised the First World War almost from its inception. The battle began barely a month after Sonny posted his letter to his home in Stanley Grove. By the time it was over it required 174 cemeteries to bury the dead on the British side alone.

In the history of Flanders Ypres had long been a focus for fighting. Incursions by Vikings, Austrian Habsburgs, Spanish inquisitors, Napoleonic French and the Dutch followed that of the Romans. Later domestic strife between weavers and cloth merchants and the peasantry and their landowners kept the cycle of conflict going. In

1914 it was the turn of the Germans to sweep into territory that had now become part of Belgium.

Already two massive First World War offensives had been launched around Ypres, the death toll from them equal to a quarter of all British servicemen killed so far in the war. Yet for all the sacrifice the results were paltry. The Germans continued to occupy the ridge above the shattered town, and the achievement of the Allies had been merely to put a bulge or 'salient' in their frontline. Like all 'salients' it meant Allied troops were surrounded by enemy guns on three sides. Every soldier who had the bad luck to be sent into the Ypres salient knew only too well that it represented little more than the jaws of a suicide trap.

Adding to the dangers was the disquieting news that Germany for some time past had been training their troops in new ways of fighting. 'They don't go over the top in waves like we do', Sonny and his comrades had been told 'but in smaller, more-compact groups. They ignore our strong points, going for the weakest and most-vulnerable parts of our line'. 'Storm troopers' was the name given to these German detachments, and its effect was to make a soldier take an even tighter grip on his rifle. Sometimes there were things you'd rather not hear about....

Although Flanders was rich in natural resources such as coal and iron ore (something that hadn't escaped the notice of colonialists who'd fought for its annexation down through the years), there was one raw material nobody much wanted though it was available in prodigious quantities: that was rain. In Flanders it rained on average every other day throughout the year. It could also be very cold and due to the region's proximity to the

North Sea, freezing fogs rolling in across the flat terrain were commonplace.

The rain and melting snow found no outlet in the flat landscape, and it didn't require a soils-specialist to confirm that the fine-grained, impermeable Flanders clay didn't drain the way other soils did. The evidence was to be seen in the water that gathered on the surface and stayed there until it evaporated or turned stagnant. Where movement did occur it was sluggish and unpredictable, the streams, drainage channels and the canals dug to carry the water away soon overflowing and in the end contributing to the flooding that took place during the wet season. Ominously for the troops in Flanders, the wet season was clearly understood to begin in late-summer.

One of the consequences of this hopeless mismatch between heaven and earth was mud – thick, glutinous mud which oozed and sucked at anything foolish enough to tangle with it. It could suck the life out of most living creatures in record time.

By all accounts however, Douglas Haig paid little heed to these precedents, ignoring even the findings of his chief intelligence guru General Charteris, who recorded: *'Careful investigation of the records of more than eighty years showed that in Flanders the weather broke early each August with the regularity of an Indian monsoon.'*

With metronomic precision Haig scheduled many of his major battles to begin and continue through periods when the weather was likely to be at its worst. The Battle of the Somme had run through the 'monsoon' period to November 1916 and Passchendaele, which began on the last day of July 1917, was to do likewise. The reports he read of the effects mud and water was having on his troops – reports recording men *'trapped to their waists'*, *'smothered'* and *'suffocated'* by the stuff – went largely ignored. In the latter stages of the Passchendaele campaign the field marshall sent his Chief of Staff, Launcelot Kiggell, to tour the swampland that had already claimed a quarter of a million casualties. *'Good God!'* Kiggell had declared, *'did we really send men to fight in this?'* His aide answered: *'You should see it further up, sir. It gets even worse...'*

Unlike previous military commanders who might have claimed they were experiencing the vicissitudes of the Flanders weather for the first time, Haig had been on the Western Front for almost three years and had no reason to plead ignorance of what might be expected. He knew what had happened at the Somme where the clay was more friable and chalky and nothing like as glutinous as in Flanders. He knew also how other battles in the region had foundered in mud, and how mud could often be as deadly as what the Germans poured out in artillery and machine-gun fire. He'd read the reports, scanned the casualty figures, been briefed and updated by his officers, and had appeared to give due weight to what they were advising. Then, Haig being Haig, ordered the battle plans to continue. That he did so should really have come as no surprise to the soldiers, especially the veteran survivors amongst them, who were manning the trenches.

The 3rd Battle of Ypres began on the 31st of July 1917, zero hour arriving predictably in a heavy shower of rain. *'The bright weather reported as coming,'* Haig wrote in his diary on the eve of battle, *'is slower than expected.'* From his post 20 miles behind the lines he could hear the rumble of artillery barrages which had begun ten days earlier: but he needed to look no further than the windows of his headquarters to see the rain sweeping in, the frequent showers now merging into a solid downpour.

For the following four days and nights the rain fell incessantly. General John Charteris was moved to say: *'Every brook is swollen and the ground is a quagmire. If it were not that all the records in previous years had given us fair warning, it would seem that Providence had declared against us.'* That thing 'Providence' again! Divine intervention it appeared was intent not on aiding the Allies but in guiding the hand of the barbarian Germans. Even Haig appeared a trifle disconsolate as reports of how the first rounds of battle were faring began landing on his desk. In a message to Lloyd George and the war cabinet, he wrote:

'The low-lying clayey soil torn by shells and sodden with rain turned to a succession of vast muddy pools. The valleys of the choked and overflowing streams were speedily transformed into long stretches of bog, impassable except for a few well-defined tracks which became marks for the enemy's artillery. In these conditions operations of any magnitude became impossible' You can imagine his dour countenance sagging even further as he handed his message over for dispatch.

Haig's plan for 3rd Ypres was to attack along a 15 mile front with around 100,000 men organised in 17 army divisions. Unknown to him however, the Germans outnumbered his troops by three divisions, although it was their disposition around the battlefields that really held the key. In broad terms the German generals focused on where their areas of strength lay rather than copying Haig's approach of packing the frontline with masses of troops. Throughout the First World War the Germans had fought defensively, relying on swift counterattacks to clear the Allies from any ground they'd had to relinquish in the opening rounds. It was to be no different at Ypres.

Although they'd increased their trench and pillbox system to six lines in the lead up to the battle, the German forward trenches were held by a light scattering of troops compared to what lay behind. Battalions of soldiers were staggered in depth throughout the rear with the strongest at the back ready to come forward when the order to counterattack was given. Retaliation was the key element, and in battlefields like those on the Western Front it had proved decisive in more cases than not. In addition, the Germans had built several hundred new machine-gun posts on the forward slopes of the ridges that the Allies were set on taking from them. The entire situation according to Haig's counterpart on the German side, Field Marshall Paul von Hindenburg, was more than satisfactory

It was with a feeling of absolute longing that we waited for the beginning of the wet season. As previous experience had taught us, great stretches of the Flemish flats would then become impassable, and even in firmer places the new shell holes would fill so quickly with ground water that men seeking shelter in them would find themselves faced with the alternative '...Shall we drown or get out of this hole?' This battle too must finally stick in the mud even though English (sic) stubbornness kept it up longer than otherwise.

Haig in contrast stuck like Flanders mud to his belief that defence presaged defeat and only 'Attack! Attack!' could guarantee victory, even if circumstances on the battlegrounds suggested otherwise. Arising from this was the commander-in-chief's personal vision...a vision that ever since the time of his first footfall on French soil had remained intact. Reduced to its barest essentials it read:

- *Allied artillery barrages to flatten the enemy's barbed-wire entanglements.*
- *Infantry over the top to take the enemy's first-line trenches.*
- *Infantry to then create gaps in the enemy's wire for cavalry to burst through.*
- *Cavalry to set about scattering the enemy's troops to the four winds.*

While the cavalry were so engaged the infantry were to continue with taking more ground, preparing for the inevitable counterattacks, and 'mopping-up' – taking care of any enemy soldiers still alive in the trenches they occupied.

At 3rd Ypres two divisions of British cavalry were already assembled to charge the Passchendaele ridge, and officers had maps showing the ground as far back as twenty miles in the German rear. The only additional feature was the instruction to link up in the end with General Rawlinson who was stationed with the Royal Navy off the Belgian coast, and who had been issued with orders to invade from the sea when the time came. Thus did Douglas Haig perceive of victory, all his faint promises of taking things *'a bite at a time'* forgotten, all the advice not to claim 3rd Ypres would win the war, cast aside.

For several weeks before the battle, army divisions, cavalry regiments, field artillery and tanks had rolled into the wrecked town of Ypres making ready to move forward to their assembly positions. The Germans watched from the surrounding ridges much as General Monash, commander of an Australian division did, but from a less elevated position:

Here comes a body of fighting troops, tin-hatted and fully equipped, marching in file into the battle area. There follows a string of perhaps one hundred motor lorries all fully loaded with supplies; a limousine motorcar with some division staff-officer; a string of regimental horse and mule drawn vehicles going up to a forward transport park; some motor-ambulance wagons...a long string of remount horses marching in twos...a great 12-inch howitzer dragged by two steam-traction engines...more infantry, thousands of them; more ambulances, more motor lorries; a long stream of Chinese coolies smart and of magnificent stature...dispatch riders on motor bikes threading their way skilfully between the gaps; a battery of artillery all fully horsed and clattering and jingling; motor lorries again heavily loaded with artillery ammunition...wagons bringing forward broken stone and road-making materials...a mounted police detachment...an antiaircraft gun, steam-motor drawn...a Royal Flying Corps car carrying parts of aeroplanes to forward hangers; more ambulances; and so on and on and on in a never-ending stream.

As in the preparations for every battle, those responsible for the logistics at 3rd Ypres were beyond criticism. Grumble as soldiers did about the lack of everything from food to ammunition, the men who prepared themselves and others for battle rarely failed to maximise the use of the resources at their command. From those who cooked and kept the troops fed, to those who carried out road repairs, organised transport and serviced the army's guns and tanks, their resource management skills combined with a dedication to duty was beyond reproach.

However, as always, when decisions on strategy had been taken everything else became purely organisational. The Germans were organised down to the last pillbox and gun emplacement: yet to suggest the British were any less prepared materially would fly in the face of fact. What was missing as the curtain rose on 3rd Ypres wasn't the orchestra, but a conductor capable of leading them.

The display of men and firepower described by General Monash would have given the assembling troops, including Sonny Boothroyd and those of the Manchester Regiment cause for optimism as they moved into position and waited for zero hour to arrive. It wasn't to last long. The Germans shelled selected targets continuously, and by night saturated the Allied trenches with mustard gas. The bedlam of exploding shells and the need to wear gas helmets at all times made sleep for the troops virtually impossible. Anxiety and exhaustion, the inseparable twins of trench life, put everyone on edge. For a young infantryman waiting for the whistle blast that would send him over the top, these were the thoughts racing through his mind as the 3rd Battle of Ypres was about to get under way:

4.15 a.m. Only ten minutes now before Zero. The horizon shows a line of grey. Dawn is coming and my heart is filled suddenly with bitterness when I realise that the day may be my last. In a few minutes we attack and we shall need all our courage and skill to drive the enemy for his trenches. A shell bursts in our trench breaking the leg of a man a few yards away. Stretcher bearers apply a dressing and carry him to the rear. 'There goes one man who won't die in the attack,' remarks a soldier almost enviously. Our company commander appears. 'Ten rounds in your magazines and fix bayonets!' he orders. There is a click of steel on steel. Only two minutes now remain. Two minutes in which a thousand thoughts mingle in my brain. The thought of the battlefield where I may lie in a few minutes weltering in blood: the sweet thought of our beloved land across the sea: and the thought of those I hold most dear. They do not know that in another moment I must face danger, even death. Yesterday, I believed I could die with something approaching indifference. Now I am aware of (an) intense desire to live. I would give anything to know beyond doubt that I had even two whole days ahead of me. Yesterday, I had made all my preparations for the voyage from which no traveller returns. But now I am unwilling to go. I see things differently than I did yesterday.

In trenches and tunnels, in shell craters and dugouts and holes scooped out of watery canal banks, the troops of many nationalities ran similar thoughts through their heads as they waited for the order to advance.

The previous evening Douglas Haig had made a visit to the headquarters of one of his senior commanders, General Sir Hubert Gough of the British Fifth Army. There he found the general, '*...in the best of spirits and full of confidence as to the results of tomorrow's fight.*' The Fifth Army, within which battalions of the Manchester Regiment formed a vital component, were to spearhead the attack on the ridges in front of Passchendaele, thereafter to push on and capture the town itself. Fighting alongside the Manchesters was to be units raised in Liverpool, all PALS originally but now so greatly depleted they had become mere remnants of an idea that had perished in the bloodshed of other battles. The rivalries between people belonging to the two cities which Lord Derby had cunningly exploited, was now revealed as a contrivance bringing benefits to neither. The prejudices that had divided people because of where they'd been born and had spent their life had now turned full circle around the unity of a battlefield graveyard.

If not a graveyard then something resembling a crypt was where Sonny Boothroyd found himself as zero hour of 3rd Ypres approached. The 19th battalion of the Manchesters were in an underground fortification called Crab Crawl Tunnel awaiting the order to surface and attack the German frontline east of Ypres. Four of the city's erstwhile PALS battalions were scheduled to fight together, Sonny's unit detailed to storm their way across the Ypres-Menin Road to their prime objective – the shattered remains of a forest identified on military maps as 'Polygon Wood.' It was a task no soldier however seasoned in warfare would have welcomed. The Germans from their fortified ridges overlooking the area had kept them firmly in their sights throughout the entire build up.

At zero hour such was the havoc already wreaked by artillery barrages – some of it caused by Allied guns firing on their own troops moving faster than the stipulated pace of 25 yards per minute – that the exits from Crab Crawl Tunnel quickly became choked with wounded men and others seeking protection in the tunnel itself. Sonny and the outgoing infantry of 'A' and 'B' companies of the 19th battalion were, in the words of the regiment's war diary, *'greatly hampered in their movements (and) only able to get out in ones and twos at a time.'* This made assembly in the open difficult to coordinate, and being still dark except where the German barrages lit up the landscape, impossible to line men up in battle formation. *'Cohesion was lost from the start,'* the diary continued, *'and (resulted in) small parties pushing out into No-Mans Land to get away from the enemy's barrage line.'* In the chaos half the officers of both companies became casualties before even crossing the British front line and the resulting loss of leadership meant further isolated groups of soldiers arriving in indeterminate numbers into the firing zone.

The fate of Sonny's brother-battalions was no less disastrous. The 16th battalion with the 18th on their right flank had assembled in an area which in places was only 50 yards from the German frontline. Where they gathered could not be dignified by the word 'trenches.' They were little more than ditches or shell and bomb holes covered with iron sheeting and streaming with water. Just as at the Somme, they soon became collecting points for disoriented attackers and wounded alike. In some cases badly injured soldiers seeking shelter in such places drowned because of being unable to move as the water levels rose.

Attempts to provide back-up support for units who'd carried out the initial attack consistently failed, and constant machine-gun fire meant the Manchesters were unable to make much headway with any of the primary objectives General Gough had set for them. Between them, the three Manchester battalions active on the first day of 3rd Ypres suffered around 700 casualties. An officer with the Anzac Corps described what he saw of them as he stumbled across one place where many of Sonny Boothroyd's comrades lay grievously hurt:

'The ridge was littered with dead, both theirs and ours. I got to one pillbox to find it just a mass of dead so passed on to the one ahead. Here I found about 50 men alive of the Manchesters. Never have I seen men so broken or demoralised. They were huddled up close behind the box in the last stages of exhaustion and fear. Fritz had been sniping them off all day and the dead and dying lay in piles. The wounded were numerous – unattended and weak, they groaned and moaned all over the place. Some had been there four days already...'

On the third day of the fruitless attack to capture Passchendaele, Sonny's unit were relieved and taken out of the line. They had spent the entire period up to their waists in mud and water. Eventually all the Manchester battalions attached to Gough's divisional army were withdrawn and sent for respite to a base camp outside the immediate danger zones. The 72 hours Sonny and his comrades had spent in the trenches had been their worst experience of the First World War so far. Muddied to the eyes, their uniforms weighed down with dirt and water, they left the battleground in no sort of recognised formation, staggering along what was left of the duck-boarding looking haggard and beastlike beneath the stubble on their cheeks. *'I have seen nothing like it,'* a captain in the medical corps wrote. *'They don't look like strong young men. They look like wounded or sick wild things.'* With them went the walking wounded, many now bereft of their soldier's equipment and carrying little more than a fresh set of nightmares. Left behind were comrades whose mutilated corpses lay in the foul clay and fetid waters of Flanders. Their names would in time be inscribed on stone: their remains in many cases would never be recovered.

It was *'hell and slaughter'* wrote a Lieutenant belonging to one of Sonny Boothroyd's fellow-Lancashire regiments after 3rd Ypres had finished. He might have added *'and to what end?'* The gains resulting from the attack on Passchendaele were by any standards a meagre return on the massive energy put into it and the ultimate cost it exacted in human life. When Haig finally ordered a halt to the carnage at the end of November 1917, the Allied frontline had advanced by little more than a mile. It resembled a tiny thumbprint on the map, a configuration that could have been taken as giving a 'thumbs-down' to Haig's willingness to sacrifice one-quarter of a million Allied troops, killed and wounded.

Today, the cost can be further assessed by counting the number of war cemeteries that crowd the area over which 3rd Ypres was fought. In a book of remembrance kept at one such cemetery a stunned visitor entered in the column provided for comments, *'None needed!'* In the sense that he meant it, he was obviously right. In other ways, of course, it could be argued that a lot more still had to be said...and was, all down the intervening decades to the present day.

Chapter 25

Sitting in Parliament, as Passchendaele floundered to a finish, were several Members of Parliament who represented Manchester constituencies during the war, including the one in which the Boothroyd family lived. Sonny's parents, Sarah and Joseph, however, didn't have any meaningful stake in influencing their decisions, or participating in what passed for democratic government. Even as late as 1914 less than 8 million people in Britain were entitled to vote in Parliamentary elections. Of those who did enjoy the privilege some seemed able to vote as many times as they cared to.

Depending on property holdings and personal wealth the 'one-man-one-vote' idea was still a distant prospect. Landowners and oligarchs alike were free to fill the ballot boxes as they saw fit. Joseph Chamberlain for example, a monocled member of the inner circle who governed colonial South Africa freely admitted to being able to vote six times in national elections, although he wasn't by any means the most privileged in this respect. Due to the carefully crafted rules applying to the registration of voters, some of Chamberlain's social class could cast up to ten votes. Presumably Chamberlain's belief that, *'the British race are [sic] the greatest of the governing races the world has ever seen...'* didn't stretch to giving many of them the means of electing their own political representatives.

John Hodge, who sat for Manchester Gorton (a working class constituency the Boothroyds had lived in for several years), was arguably the most ardent pro-war member of the House of Commons. At one time President of both the steelworkers union and the TUC, he attacked fellow Labour Party colleagues for even considering a negotiated peace with the Germans, his anger rising to incandescence when hearing that some unions were planning to go on strike during the war. Industrial action at such times, he declared, should be viewed as treason attracting the full weight of the law. The law on treason at the time allowed judges, if they so chose, to don the black cap and pass sentence of execution. Hodge became Minister of Labour in 1916 and Lloyd George moved him on to Pensions the following year. So dedicated was he to the war, that in the election held after the Armistice the Conservatives declined to oppose him and he was returned to Parliament with a massive majority of those eligible to vote. To the surprise of no one, in 1926 Hodge was at the forefront in attacking the General Strike.

Not to be outdone in the patriot game were two other erstwhile working men who vied with each other to be Hodge's lieutenants at Westminster. John Clynes, a former child-worker in the textile mills and previously full-time organiser for the Lancashire Gas Workers Union, was MP for North-east Manchester - a constituency that contained some of the worst slums in Europe. So loyal was Clynes to the War Cabinet's resolution to keep on 'hitting, hitting' at the Germans and fighting on to the bitter end, that Lloyd George rewarded him with control of the Ministry of Food in 1917. What Seymour Mead made of that can only be guessed at. Rationing rather rationalism was to be Clynes's main contribution to First World War politics.

Shoulder to shoulder with him however, was Ben Tillet the former dockers champion whose seat was North Salford – a town sharing a common boundary with Manchester. Tillet's enthusiasm for bombing German civilians and punishing pacifists at home saw him comfortably elected as an 'Independent' by the relatively few people eligible to vote for him. To them it showed how far the man who'd risked jail and blacklisting in 1899 over a pay claim (known as the 'docker's tanner') had reneged on what they had viewed as his dangerously socialistic ideals. Now Tillet tramped the country urging industrial workers to join the armed forces and criticising anyone in the Labour Party who was inclined to see the First World War as having imperialist and internationalist dimensions.

Of the others who claimed to represent the unenfranchised folk of Sonny Boothroyd's Manchester, only their names and their support for the conflict rather than their reputations have survived. Two knights of the realm (both Liberals), a businessman, and a private-school educated solicitor (both Conservatives), made up the rest of the city's MPs who between 1908 and the start of the First World War were elected and re-elected with serial monotony, in several cases returned to Parliament with the help of their 'rivals', unopposed.

At one point C.P. Scott, owner and editor of the Manchester Guardian had been a Manchester M.P. as was

Winston Churchill. Both were portrayed as idiosyncratic figures, non-conforming individuals who beat their own tracks through life whatever anyone had to say. Churchill took his bath and water heater with him on the bit of short-lived soldiering he did on the Western Front: Scott was a ken speckle figure travelling to his office through the city streets pedalling a large upright bicycle. Neither man however, displayed any eccentricities when it came to giving their support to the war. Churchill resigned his post in government after taking flak for the First World War fiasco in Gallipoli, but was never less than ardent about defeating the Germans. In the columns of his newspaper, Scott wrote: *I am strongly of the opinion that the war ought not to have taken place and that we ought not to have become parties to it: but once in it the whole future of our nation is at stake and we have no choice but to do the utmost we can to secure success.* It was the sort of declaration designed to have his employees looking for their nearest recruiting centre, which his chief leader writer at the Guardian, C.E. Montagu, {the man you'll remember who blackened his hair to fool the recruiting officers} wasted little time in doing. It would have been scant consolation however, for the Boothroyds to know that their German counterparts had about as much stake in democracy as they had, despite all men over 25 in that country having the right to vote. The Junkers, with their huge landed estates and neo-feudal approaches to governing society, had seen to that. The German constitution, drawn-up carefully to maximise Prussian power and control, viewed Parliamentary representation as a necessary evil entirely subordinate to the autocratic rule of the Kaiser. Industrialisation and the demands of the new, urbanised population would never be allowed to reach a level that threatened to undermine Junkers power. In 1905 the Kaiser had made it clear no 'external war' – by which he meant stabilising Europe around a new German Empire – would ever be possible if liberalism and democracy was allowed to develop. He stated that shooting, beheading and 'de-fanging' should be the price paid by anyone espousing views to the contrary.

As it turned out he needn't have worried. German socialists effectively defanged themselves in 1914 when a major part of the German Social Democratic Party (SDP) led by Friedrich Ebert, voted almost unanimously in favour of the war declaring it necessary for the patriotic defence of the Fatherland. Like Tillet, Hodge and Clynes, Ebert was a former trade unionist, the son of a poor tailor and a saddle-maker to trade. For a brief period after the Kaiser abdicated, he became the first President of the new German Republic.

In Germany, left-wing parties like the communists were tolerated only if they observed the blanket ban on holding meetings and publishing their views. In Britain, Labour MPs were accepted into Parliament but regarded as an insignificant minority, the mass of the people who might have voted for more of them having no vote. In both countries the oligarchs continued to hold on tight to the reins of power, the titled landowners of one evenly matched to their Junkers counterparts in the other. Attempts to describe one as being more venomous, more illiberal and more hostile to democratic ideas than the other amounted to no more than ruminating on which is better, being gagged by a strip of adhesive tape or a silk scarf.

In the First World War trenches the troops were told little or nothing of how the war was progressing overall, and in Parliament MPs were told only what the War Cabinet wanted them to hear. The newspapers plugged away with the propaganda fed to them by the War Office Press Bureau and others, and by 1917 the democratic deficit was at its zenith in both Britain and Germany. The pools of patriotism were made to appear unruffled unlike those that gathered for the likes of Sonny Boothroyd on the flat, painful fields of Flanders.

Chapter 26

The soldier immediately in front of Sonny loses his footing on the icy duckboards and crashes into the side of the trench. Instinctively, Sonny makes a grab for his tumbling rifle. Closer to you than your mother, the military have told him, is your rifle. Even in battle, stopping for a fallen comrade is only permissible if the sole intention is retrieving his weapons. Anything else, it is said, will be dealt with by other people following in the rear.

The man curses and regains his balance checking as he plods on that the rest of his equipment is still intact. Among the assortment of items strapped to his body are several belts of ammunition, a couple of hand grenades, two white flares and a set of wire cutters. A filled water bottle and his trenching tool add to the weight of the haversack he carries between his shoulders – a canvas bag containing more things to be hefted, including the unconsumed portion of his iron rations. In this war a soldier seldom goes anywhere light of step, or light of heart.

In making the sudden motion to help the stumbling soldier, Sonny has only helped resurrect the pain in his shoulder. It's a pain that has never really departed since he sustained a shrapnel wound on being returned to the trenches after his battalion's first disastrous engagement with Paschendaele. As a result his next contact with his mother in Manchester came by way of a Field Services Postcard sent from a Casualty Clearing Station behind the lines. As communication went, the message it contained didn't amount to much, and what Sarah Boothroyd made of it can only be guessed at. A Field Services Postcard was fugitively brief consisting of just three short sentences:

'I am quite well.'
'I have your letter of...'
'My letter follows at first opportunity.'

Along the bottom was printed a clear message from the military. *'Anything else added and this postcard will be destroyed.'* Anything else included even the tiniest hint of the nature or extent of a soldier's injuries.

At least Sonny's postcard provided his mother with some alleviation of her anxiety: knowing he was alive however, had to be balanced against her ignorance of his whereabouts and the exact nature of the wounding that had caused his hospitalisation.

Sonny's whereabouts, at least for a period after September 10th 1917, was mostly Kemmel Hill – the highest point on the entire Flanders plain – where the 19th battalion were detailed to provide ridge defences. Even here however, his infantry unit wasn't free from persistent enemy attacks. Paschendale continued to grind on and during daylight hours sniper fire and shelling made troop movements perilous. At night there were trench raids to contend with.

In November the battalion was moved again, this time to more ridge defence work east of the town of Zillebeke where Sonny joined them after his discharge from hospital. By early December still pained and plastered he was back in a support role at the Hedge Street Tunnels. This at least provided some time for scrawling a further letter to Stanley Grove, even if its content, either because of self-censoring or just war weariness, appeared disjointed and lacking in logical thought.

Pte. J. Boothroyd 18452
December 11th 1917.

Dear mother...just a line to let you know I received your parcel yesterday which I was very glad of. I also received Eva's letter. I am always glad to hear from home. I am not feeling so bad lately. I am writing this letter in the line so you must excuse the writing. I had my photo taken about two weeks ago. The fellow what took them has been paralysed and his camera broke in about 18 pieces. I suppose it was the shock. The other lad is a Leicester lad. He was out in Ireland scrapping with the Sin Fiens (sic). What do you think about them? Are they any good? Well, mother I can't say much I couldn't say when we come home. So cheer up. I hope you have a Merry Christmas and a Bright and Prosperous New Year.
With best wishes and fondest love to all.
Sonny.
Alfred xxxxxx   Bertha xxxxxx xxxxxxxxx

Not long into the New Year Sonny's 22nd birthday would hove into view. He'd already spent two birthdays in uniform, one eclipsed by his preparations for the Somme the other similarly overshadowed by Arras. Surely, he told himself, I can't spend another birthday in these conditions!

Like all battle hardened soldiers however, he's learnt not to look much further ahead than the next detail although tonight he would have been surprised if his fellow infantrymen had not let thoughts of the battalion's delayed Christmas dinner drift through their minds. Maybe a few surprises were in store. Perhaps their officers for once would don the aprons and take turns at waiting on their subordinates. If a Christmas bird with all the trimmings wasn't likely to materialise, then who's to say a bottle or two of something other than rum wouldn't make their appearance?

Sonny had heard the battalion they were about to relieve would be returning to some sort of festive affair where food and drink beyond the usual dismal fare was bound to surface. The news of this had naturally been greeted by his comrades with the customary pique. *'So long as the buggers haven't scoffed the lot before we get back,' a soldier had growled. 'If they 'ave they'll wish the fuckin' Bosche had got 'em before I did!'*

All thoughts of Christmas however, must now be set aside as Sonny reaches the first of the supply trenches where men will peel off under instructions from one of the officers in charge of the relief operation. It has just gone six-thirty and darkness in Flanders is complete. The officer commanding Sonny's unit is 2nd Lieutenant Smith - a small, wiry individual who is totally focused on what's expected of him this evening. He raises his hand beckoning Sonny forward. All speech is now strictly forbidden so the message is not easy to decipher in the darkness. Sonny hesitates for a moment peering into the gloom but he needs nothing in the way of enhanced night-vision to identify what he first sees as shapes coming over the parapet of the trench. They are certainly out of place, and the speed and determination with which they drop to the duckboards enables Sonny to recognise them only too well. The next thing he's aware of is that the raiding party of Germans are upon him……

For several minutes, chaos reigns. Either side of Sonny soldiers are yelling, falling out of line, grabbing for anything that might quickly become a weapon. The 21-inch sword bayonet fixed to their rifles is virtually useless in close-quarters combat such as this - too long, too cumbersome, yet safer than firing off rounds. In the mayhem you might shoot one of your comrades rather the enemy. Some men have honed the blade of their trenching tool to razor sharpness. With a single stroke it could almost decapitate an assailant. Others wield clubs, self-styled wooden affairs made from close-grained solid oak. Yet others resort simply to using the stock of their rifle as a bludgeoning instrument.

The Germans however, are better prepared. Pistols, stick bombs, hand grenades - the element of surprise in trench raids requires much advanced planning. They drop to the trench bottom unencumbered by heavy greatcoats and stuffed haversacks. They are a tried and tested team, have practised for events such as this many times over. They've pinpointed with accuracy where the gaps are in the barbed-wire, measured them, charted them, built their raiding plans around them. Just three weeks previously they'd done a dummy run when Sonny's unit was carrying out a relief operation exactly like the one now in progress. Every man jack of them knows his role and plays it with precision.

A soldier of the 19th battalion sends up a white flare – a message telling others they are being attacked, a message calling for help. Until its light fades the flare holds the surrounding trenches in its magnesium glare. For a few seconds men appear frozen in time, etched into a background of grim desolation. Something crashes into the face of 2nd Lieutenant Smith, knocking him sideways so that he collides with the trench wall and slithers to the ground. Men grapple with each other either side of his inert body. Smith hears their cries, their curses, smells the familiar stench of human combat and fear. Shots ring out, pistol shots, softer and not so ear-splitting, but just as deadly as those from a rifle.

Another flare swooshes into the night sky. Lieutenant Smith manages to turn his head and sees he is not the only casualty of the raid. Nearby another figure in khaki lies prone, his life's-blood oozing away between the slats of the duckboards. Smith tries to see who the man is, but the soldier's head is turned away from him. Gradually the noises around him recede. The scrape of hurrying boots on the trench parapet above him are also quick to depart. Yet another flare rises into the night sky. Then its light is extinguished and the all-enveloping darkness returns.....

Chapter 27

A clamping cold has taken possession of Manchester. It makes people hurry along the streets, heading for work, heading for the shops, heading for the ever-lengthening food queues the war has brought to the city. Even the smoke from the factories appears reluctant to leave the warmth of its enclosing brickwork and spreads itself low and flat across the rooftops. It has been like this since subdued church bells rang in the new year of 1918.

A postman comes down the Stockport Road blowing into his hands as he walks. He is an elderly man, called out of retirement to do the job normally done by a younger person now conscripted by the army. It's a familiar story. Women are driving the trams: boys are barrowing goods: a generation of old folks and disabled ex-servicemen are helping to keep the city ticking over and will continue to do so until someone, somewhere decides enough is enough and the war must now end.

The postman makes his deliveries at many of the retail stores gathered around the junction with Stanley Grove, including Seymour Mead where he is glad for the brief respite granted by the shop's relatively warm interior. Then he continues to the next call on his round – a house that is sandwiched between a railway bridge and more shops forming the eastern sweep of the Stockport Road into Stanley Grove itself. He's already taken the buff-coloured envelope out of his bag before walking up to the front door. Pushing it through the letterbox he gives a couple of soft knocks on the wood panel and moves quickly away. He has made so many deliveries of this sort over the past 18 months that he no longer wants to be associated with them. By the time the family inside the house have responded to his knocking the postman, despite his advanced years, has disappeared into the distance.

The envelope pushed through the door is addressed to Sarah Boothroyd and is without markings save for the letters O.H.M.S. (On His Majesty's Service) stamped on the top left-hand corner. Sarah will never be able to recall if it was she who recovered it from the doormat or one of her children who brought it to her, unopened. All she will ever remember was the message she found inside.

Mrs. Sarah Boothroyd
3 Stanley Grove
Longsight Manchester

Dear Madam
It is with deep sympathy that I write to you to inform you that your son No.18452 Pte. Joseph Boothroyd having been killed in action was today buried in a military cemetery well behind the line.
I trust it will be some consolation to you to know he was buried with great respect, and with full rights of the Church conducted by the chaplain. A cross will be

erected and I can assure you that everything has been done to commemorate the memory of your son.

Burial Officer
30th Division
30. 12. 17.

Sarah reads and rereads the letter without sitting down. The burial officer's signature is scrawled illegibly across the bottom, as incoherent to her as the cause of the pain that's risen to impose its icy grip around her chest. She takes the letter through to the kitchen where other members of the Boothroyd family wait. Sarah holds the letter in one hand, the envelope in the other. Her hand trembles setting the flimsy papers astir as though caught in a sudden draught: but words won't come because words are irrelevant. No one needs to ask what has happened because no one is in any doubt what the answer will be. Even Bertha...*particularly* Bertha...is able to read the anguish signalling from deep within her mother's eyes.......

On the day following arrival of the burial officer's letter the postman delivers another. This time it is the Army Records Office in nearby Preston writing to confirm that Sonny is dead – 'Killed in Action':

'By His Majesty's command I am to forward the enclosed message of sympathy from Their Gracious Majesties the King and Queen. I am at the same time to express the regret of the Army Council at the soldier's death in his Country's service.'

The enclosed message from Buckingham Palace reads simply *'I join with my grateful people in sending you this memorial of a brave life given for others in the Great War.'* It was signed, this time legibly...George Rex.

In time the Boothroyds were to receive three medals commemorating Sonny's war service. One of them, around four inches in diameter, was to become known as the 'Death Penny.' In cities and towns across Britain, a significant fortune in 'Death Pennies' rolled their way to more front doors than would ever be counted. However, the Boothroyds like most families never displayed the medals. Tokens of valour were no replacement for a dead husband or son, and in many cases both. The medals stayed unsullied in the boxes they were delivered in.

Friends and relatives of the Boothroyds came to offer their sympathy and share the family's grief: but the death of yet another soldier had become too commonplace for people to grieve as intensely as the family enduring the pain. In normal times sons expected to bury their parents: in this war the opposite had become the case. The only difference for Sarah and Joseph was they never got anywhere close to attending the committal of their son's remains to the earth. Long before the time came for Sonny to die the military had ceased to repatriate the corpses of fallen soldiers. It wasn't only the cost involved or the magnitude of the task in terms of resources, or indeed the impossibility of finding the acreages needed to bury so many people: it was also the effects on the population at home of the spectacle of so much death in their midst.

Within a few weeks details arrived of Sonny's grave in Bedford House cemetery at Zillebeke, east of Ypres. The letter described what would appear on his headstone – his name, his regiment, the badge of his army unit and the emblem of his religious faith which for most British soldiers was a plain crucifix. A space was to be left at the foot of the headstone for a short personal inscription whose choice of words were to be left to his family. The number of words and letters used however were to be strictly limited and for each chiselled letter the cost would be three-and-a-half pennies. The price to pay was beyond the means of most families, including the Boothroyds. As a result, no added inscription was ever carried out on Sonny's burial stone.

Like many bereaved mothers Sarah Boothroyd sought to assuage her grief by turning to spiritualism rather than the traditions of her Church of England upbringing. By the latter stages of the First World War the established churches were attracting growing criticism over their unequivocal support for the conflict. As the war continued to exact its toll religious platitudes were palpably failing to lessen the anguish of bereaved families. Being told that Sonny was now in the *'Arms of the Lord'* was little comfort to his mother, and she joined the growing congregations that looked to making contact with the dead through a psychic medium. If nothing else spiritualism became an analgesic for the torment Sarah endured in the period following her son's death.

In a few weeks time the post brought further correspondence relating to Sonny's demise. In this case it came in the form of a scroll emblazoned with the Royal coat of arms. Above Sonny's name and regiment was written:

He whom this scroll commemorates was numbered among those who, at the call of King and Country, left all that was dear to them, endured hardness, faced danger, and finally passed out of the sight of men by the path of duty and self-sacrifice, giving up their own lives that others may live in freedom.

It was a sentence...a single sentence...whose words seemed to stretch further across the page than the lives of those who qualified for its issue. Below it was written the command:

Let those who come after see to it that his name be not forgotten.

The postman who delivered it to 3 Stanley Grove however, might have been excused for being amongst the first to experience forgetfulness. He was heading along the cold streets of Manchester his shift not even half-over. In his bag lay more than a few similar mailings still to be delivered...

Chapter 28
Post-War

Sonny was buried three days after being killed in the grounds of a small chateau once surrounded by parkland and woods, but which soon became part of the war-shattered remains which characterised the entire area around the village of Zillebeke. In true 'naming-is-possession' fashion the British who'd occupied Chateau Rosendal for most of the war had renamed it Bedford House, so that Sonny's last resting place became Bedford House Cemetery. They couldn't name many of the soldiers who lay beside him, however: in some areas of the burial ground up to two-thirds of the occupants were unable to be identified at the time of their internment.

Although Sarah Boothroyd had been informed of Sonny's death, there was no hint as to how he'd died other than the only too familiar 'Killed in Action.' That mystery remains. His battalion's diary for the day - Boxing Day 1917 - records the injury to 2nd Lieutenant Smith but fails to put names to other casualties of the trench raid which took place on that day. Had Sonny been dispatched by a bullet? Did he sustain a fatal blow to the head? Or had he been caught in the malevolent blast of a stick bomb thrown by a departing German indifferent to the havoc it would cause? It is unlikely we will ever know. Even his assailant would be unaware of what he had wrought. All we can say is that Sonny probably died immediately and did not experience the slow and often obscene death many of his comrades had endured before his. Although his mother was supplied with the details of Sonny's location within the cemetery where he lay, it is unlikely she or any other member of the Boothroyd family ever had the resources to visit his grave.

Had he survived to attain his 22nd year of life and beyond, Sonny would have been returned home like thousands of First World War soldiers after the Armistice had been signed. In the trenches during the latter part of the conflict, a song (sung to the tune of 'What a Friend we have in Jesus') seemed to express their disenchantment with the whole futile business of fighting. Its first verse was:

When this bloody war is over,
Oh, how happy I will be,
When I get my civvy clothes back.
No more soldiering for me.

What they met with after returning to 'hearth and home' however, was very far removed from what they would have imagined. '*The 1914 men were treated very badly after the war,*' said one demobilised and disillusioned member of the infantry. '*They bluffed us with that saying, 'A land fit for heroes to live in.' You had to have a limb off to keep your pension – if you had any wounds you were finished. If two limbs were missing you got thirty-three shillings per week and it went down from there.'*

He went on to say that many returning soldiers ended up at the labour exchange in a fruitless search for jobs, living meanwhile on what the state provided:

I got twenty-nine shillings a week for three months, then a pound, and after six months it was dropped to seventeen shillings. There were two million unemployed, and big fellows with all their limbs couldn't find a job....

Another survivor kept a record of what happened to a British soldier when he was repatriated to his homeland. The military paid a £15 war gratuity, £5 a year for every year of service, four weeks pay for leave and a ration allowance. He also received a clothing allowance from which one pound was deducted if he chose to keep his army greatcoat. If not, and he handed it in, the one-pound was returned to him. By contrast senior army officers fared much better, Douglas Haig for example, being given an earldom, an estate in the Scottish Borders and a tax-free golden handshake of £100,000 – a fortune in those days by anyone's standards.

Faced with few options many more-youthful soldiers chose to re-enlist with the armed forces, becoming part of the post-war cohorts sent to 'police' British possessions abroad such as Ireland where they augmented units like the Black & Tans – a force fighting the Irish peoples' demand for independence.

In some ways the war forced politicians into making changes which were to be built on in the years to follow. Women like Sarah Boothroyd aged thirty and over were given the vote in Parliamentary elections, and an extension to the school-leaving age was introduced. As a direct outcome to the wounding, maiming and disease inflicted on so many, nursing was finally recognised as a profession and plastic surgery including facial reconstruction made significant strides in the treatment of war casualties. But the land fit for heroes continued to elude most people. Germany was bankrupt and the war reparations demanded of it which was to finance Britain's recovery proved impossible – as empty a promise as much as the 'land fit for heroes' was. Neither was the First World War 'the war to end all wars.' In no time at all a second world war was to be unleashed demonstrating how armistices, treaties like that at Versailles in 1920 and other agreements were just truces…mere pauses…between renewed strife and bloodshed.

One survivor of the First World War – a civilian-in-khaki who'd been a weaver before enlisting with the 9th battalion of the Manchester Regiment – said afterwards *'they came close to making a cripple of me, but I'm still here. Nearly all the others have gone. Why?'*

By 'why?' he was referring of course to the fact that he'd been spared when so many had perished. Put another way however, the question is even more relevant. On Judgement Day, if such a day comes, the ground will open within the girdle of graves created by the First World War and there will be many soldiers stepping forth only too keen for an answer to the question of why they died at all.

Postscript

Towards the end of the 1970s a Manchester woman called Mildred Beech helped a relative of hers move out of his house and into a nursing home. The old man, now in his eighties, had become too frail to live on his own and fairly soon after moving he died, leaving Mildred to deal with the business of disposing of the contents of his home. However, before she could get around to dealing with that the house was broken into and vandalised. Among the debris Mildred found scattered across the floor of an upstairs room was sheets of paper which she set about gathering up. When she found time to go through them she discovered they consisted of two sets of related documents – one set official, government-type documents: the other letters written in a neat sloping hand on paper that was stained as much by mud and grime as it was by the boot of the vandal. They were of course, the letters written by Sonny Boothroyd to his mum from the trenches of World War One.

The man who had kept Sonny's letters close to him for over sixty years was Alfred Boothroyd, Sonny's kid brother, and the house which had been vandalised was No.3 Stanley Grove where Alfred had lived all of his life.

Mildred was his niece and the daughter of Eva Boothroyd, which also made Sonny her uncle. As she read through his letters and perused the accompanying documents relating to his death, she realised the vandals had left something more-valuable to the current generation of Boothroyds than they could ever have imagined. Although there was no sign of Sonny's medals after the break-in, including the 'Death Penny' which the vandals had probably stolen, by just holding his letters in her hand seemed to connect her to someone she'd never known in a way few things ever could. It was like the feeling one gets when touching an antiquity, an object made by someone long gone and forgotten but somehow able to be drawn close because of an object distinctively fashioned by their own hand. It was one reason among several that made Mildred feel obliged to hold on to her uncle's letters.

For a time she kept Sonny's letters safe in her own keeping without having much idea of what she could possibly do with them. Eventually, she passed them to my brother and his partner who are peace activists and friends of hers. They in turn gave them to me on the assumption that I might be able to do something with them, knowing I had an incorrigible habit of writing stuff that other people who were capable of making mistakes, published from time to time in newspapers and magazines. I agreed to try, although it took a while for me to come up with the idea of turning Sonny's letters into a script for radio.

I wasn't too unfamiliar at the time with writing scripts, having penned a one-act play that had done the rounds at the Edinburgh Link Festival, and a couple of short stories that had been broadcast by BBC Radio 4 but my first attempt at interesting the BBC in the script I eventually wrote about Sonny, failed miserably. According to Radio Scotland, my first port of call being a Scot, Sonny's letters *'would not sustain the listener's interest'* and so was not suitable for broadcasting. It was the most-damning criticism any writer could ever receive: but as usually happens in such cases, it only strengthened my determination to make progress with it.

I immediately turned the script around and sent it to the BBC's headquarters in London where, thanks to someone I'll never know, spotted its direct relevance to Manchester, and unlike my fellow-countrymen at Radio Scotland, sent it there for consideration. Soon, BBC Radio Manchester was in touch inviting me to the city with the express aim of turning my work into a programme.

When I got there I found a senior producer at the station buzzing with ideas as to how he would arrange my script for broadcast. He was Alex Greenalgh and he proposed a half-hour programme that stuck with the structure of my story (that being an actor playing Sonny reading aloud his letters from the trenches, and a narrator who set them in the context of Sonny's involvement with the First World War), but with certain innovations that would embellish and enhance the script. Chief amongst these was the idea of fading the end of Sonny's story into the Last Post followed by a brass band playing the popular hymn 'The Day Thou Givest Lord Hath Ended.' As it turned out the programme when it was eventually broadcast proved to be a big success, not least because of Alex's imaginative treatment of my script.

The programme went out on Remembrance Day 1981 under the title I had chosen for it, *'Just a Few Lines.'* It was broadcast to coincide with the remembrance service at London's cenotaph which began at eleven in the morning. When it was over BBC Radio Manchester received a flood of phone calls from people asking for a tape of the programme saying how moving they had found it. One of the callers was Mildred Beech, but the BBC was not resourced to provide the tapes requested so instead offered to repeat the programme on the evening of the same day, which they duly did encouraging listeners to make their own recording of it. I was naturally pleased by the outcome, especially so because it honoured not just Sonny Boothroyd but in a sense all those of a similar mien who'd perished in the First World War. With that thought in mind I left it there, believing that what I'd set out to do had been accomplished. As it turned out, I was wrong.

A few months later I received a note from Alex Greenalgh saying that, *'Just a Few Lines'* had been put forward for a Sony Award – a rather prestigious trophy – for the best radio programme in its category, which it subsequently won. *'I knew it was good,'* Alex wrote in his usual irascible way *'but not that good!'* I was told the award came as a scroll, but when I naively asked when it would be sent to me, Alex informed me bluntly that the scroll was meant to hang on the wall of his office not in mine. *'If you need to prove it to anybody,'* he added *'just show them this letter with my signature.'* He also enclosed a studio tape of the programme which I have kept by me ever since, much as Alfred Boothroyd did with Sonny's letters.

At the Sony Awards ceremony which I couldn't attend because of work commitments, I learned later the Director of the BBC at the time – a man called Aubrey

Singer – had commented that, *'Just a Few Lines'* ought to be considered as base material for a book, although he failed to say if BBC Publications would consider publishing it! Nevertheless, it was encouragement enough for me to ponder the possibility of doing just that. However, despite much 'pondering' over the years to come increased responsibilities at work combined with the need to help my wife raise a couple of small children prevented me making a start on any such book: until now that is.

A few years ago I decided to give up full-time employment and devote more of my energy to writing. Almost the first project I embarked on was this book, which involved much research and travel to Sonny's home town of Manchester where I met-up with Mildred Beech who supplied much-valued background information on the Boothroyd family. I am indebted as much to her as I am to you dear reader. It is not my book now but yours, to make of it what you will. I hope you find it worthwhile.